Telling the Truth

The Life and Times of
the British Honduran
Forestry Unit
in Scotland (1941-44)

by Amos A. Ford

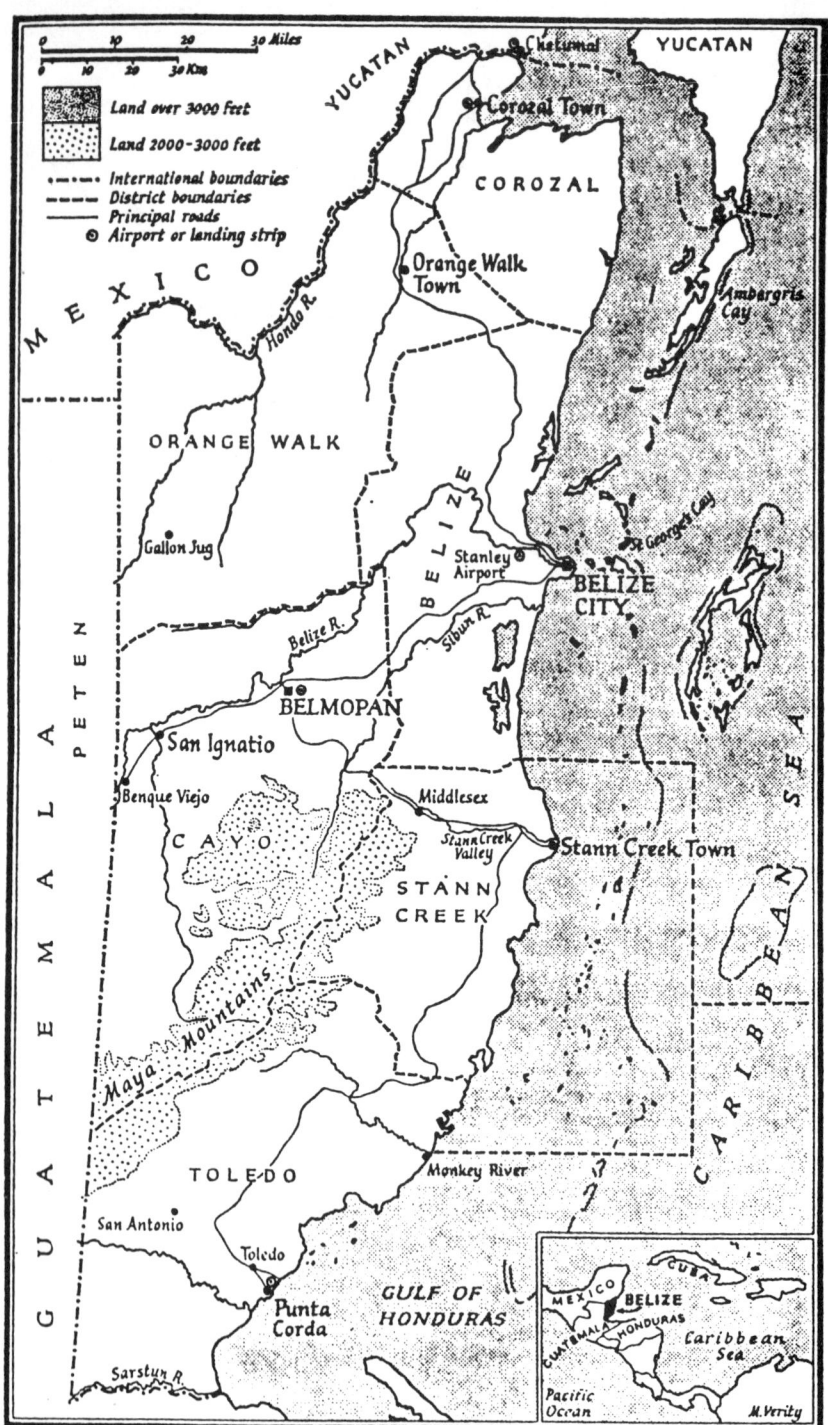

BELIZE

Telling the Truth

The Life and Times of
the British Honduran Forestry Unit in Scotland (1941-44)

by Amos A. Ford

Karia Press

Telling The Truth:
The Life and Times of
The British Honduran Forestry Unit
in Scotland, 1941-44.

First published by **Karia Press** in 1985.

Copyright © Amos A. Ford, 1984.

Photoset in Times 10/11 by Ros and Mel.
Book and cover design concept and design by Buzz Johnson
Photos courtesy Amos Ford
Printed by Whitstable Litho Ltd., Kent.

ISBN 0 946918 02 1 Pbk
ISBN 0 946918 03 1 Hbk

Distributed by **Karia Press**
BCM Karia Press
London W.C.1N 3XX

Contents

On the Author i
Foreword iii
The Author's Personal Contribution to the War Effort v
Publisher's Note vii
Acknowledgements ix

1 An Introduction to Belize in History
2 The Call, Response and Preparations 7
3 The First Contingent 17
4 The Western Atlantic: The Journey Continues 29
5 The Second Forestry Contingent of 1942 48
6 The Camps 57
7 Conflict Between Departments and Management 63
8 Outside the Camps 72
9 Disbandment of the BHFU (1943) 76
10 The Ellis Island Experience (August 1943) 81
11 Conclusion 84
   Appendix 88

On The Author

The Author, Amos Ford, was born in Belize City on November 15th 1916. His early education was at the Baptist and Wesleyan Methodist Schools. After leaving school at the age of 16, he worked both in Belize itself and in many other countries; between 1933 and 1939 he travelled and worked in Central American countries, including Mexico, Honduras, and Guatemala. On his return to Belize in 1940 he volunteered to go to the U.K., to do essential warwork, and joined the British Honduran Forestry Unit. His group of the first contingent arrived in Scotland in October, 1941.

Following the disbandment of the Unit in 1943, Mr Ford found a job, still on Essential War Work, at the Newcastle Breweries Ltd. in Newcastle-on-Tyne. He later worked with the London and North Eastern Railways before securing a Government Grant to study Advanced Accounts on a full-time basis at Constantine Technical College, Middlesbrough, during the year 1946/1947.

On successful completion of the course – and after a month of unemployment – he was recruited as a temporary Civil Servant at the Longbenton office of the Ministry of National Insurances. He remained there until 1960 when he moved south to London where he regained employment in the Ministry. He retired from the Department of Health & Social Security – the new name of the old M.N.I. – in March, 1980.

Mr. Ford is an accomplished musician specialising in playing the Spanish Guitar. He has played in bands and has given public performances at concerts, night spots, etc., in Tyneside and London. He also conducts classes in the playing of the instrument.

ii   On the Author

In addition, he has been in community affairs, with an emphasis on the problems arising from racism in British society. Mr Ford has, since 1977, been researching and writing historical and autobiographical works.

He also studied for a diploma in Economics at the University of London which was to be of much use to him in many fields of voluntary activities including discussion with Members of Parliament concerning the current dispute between H.M. Government and the Republic of Guatemala in trying to keep that dispute before the eyes and attention of the British public.

Foreword

In writing this Book, I have been at pains to verify all sources of information in order that a 'balanced' presentation may be possible. I have interviewed ex-members of the British Honduras Forestry Unit, in order that the picture portrayed by the book may be fair and accurate as far as is humanly possible.

It is for that reason that I have quoted so extensively (verbatim) from the official records at the Public Records Office at Kew, in Richmond, Surrey, England. The authorities employers seemed to be in the habit of 'by-passing' in their records, matters which do not reflect favourably on their management of affairs. At the same time, they are not slow in pointing out all the faults and misconducts – real or imagined – of the workers from the Caribbean.

It is this one-sided recording of history which this book has set out to correct the picture from the foresters point of view before the general public. Throughout, the Black foresters, unlike the forestry contingents from Australia, Canada, Newfoundland and others were made to appear most unsavoury and worthless to say the least. For the writer, who was an active participant as a member of the British Honduran Forestry Unit (B.H.F.U.) the official records made disturbing reading.

Thus, the reader is asked to bear with the author as he tries to capture the spirit and motivating forces at work vis-a-vis the B.H.F.U. and the Ministry of Supply in 1941 to 1944 in particular. In contrast to this negative portrayal of the men from British Honduras, one extract from a report on the Newfoundland Forestry Unit (reference AVIA/22/1352 P.R.O.) will suffice.

Foreword

> "I should like to make you a brief report on my recent visit to the Newfoundland Forestry Unit camps and to give you some idea of my reactions since last I visited the camps in 1942.
>
> I was particularly struck with the excellent spirit of the men; they seemed contented and happy in spite of having worked for over four years at a job which many of them would have liked to have changed for one of more active contact with the enemy during the war.
>
> I found them determined to give their best and to see it through to the end. The amenities of the camps had much improved. All the canteens I visited were clean and well kept. Bright posters on the walls added a certain gaiety to the interiors.
>
> A new feature which I noted since my last visit was the provision of eduction huts attached to each canteen. I was given to understand that the Newfoundlanders welcomed this innovation and made considerable use of these opportunities for study."

This report is in significant contrast to those prepared on the condition of the men 'from Equitorial America' — to use the phrase coined by the Duke of Buccleuch in his several comments and observations on the British Honduras Forestry Unit.

Amos Ford
May, 1984

The Author's Personal Contribution To The War Effort

My own contribution to the production of timber was, as a 'scaler'. This was a minor officer who was responsible for the work done in the forest by the men. Each Scaler had a number of men under his control and for whose production of timber he was responsible at the end of each day.

Armed with a tape-measure, a note-book and a measuring instrument known as a 'Calliper', I boarded a truck with about twelve men and proceeded to the forest where the men would be allotted their respective task of felling the timber. In my turn, I had to keep a record of the amount of timber (cubic content) felled or the cubic quantity computed by the scaler on each man's behalf. For this task, the scaler received his usual weekly wages plus a bonus calculated on the total quantity of timber felled, or on the total cubic quantity of timber produced for the week.

At other times, I was to take a number of men to a given forest where they would load the truck with logs or pulp-wood to meet the invoiced demand of a particular industry or business, including the coal mines, which used a lot of pit-props to shore up mine tunnels, etc.

It was a cold task because one was working in the open, high up on a Scottish hillside where the timber was located in most cases.

Travelling in the open uncovered trucks in the icy winter mornings was itself, a daunting experience! With the vehicle moving fast over the road, ensuring that it did not become a German raider's target, the very cold winds were more than our tropical bodies could stand at times. This was, more often than not, the cause of much absenteeism as some of the men could not take it and dodged work. Many were taken before a magistrate on Essential Works Ordinance charge. Those found guilty were fined.

To Belizean mahogany cutters, the little – or rather miniscule – nature of the timber they had to fell in Scotland, compared to the huge size of a mahogany tree, made the timber seem no more than broom-sticks to them, and they devoured the forests in no time. Yet we were called 'low producers' which is difficult to understand. We had new and very severe weather conditions to contend with, lack of official attention, illness and of course, the level of poor food provided surely must have all added to how good or bad we performed or were seen by an indifferent ministry of supply.

As the records do not show the workers' total output for any period we shall never know the real situation vis-a-vis their contribution to the total timber felled between 1941 and 1943.

Publisher's Note

We do not usually come across historical works written by people who themselves have experienced the events. This contribution by Amos Ford is published for many reasons. Among these we note the relevance of the subject matter in both charting the history of Black people in Britain and understanding the racism meted out.

With great humility the publication is presented. It is one of the results of a struggle to publish and that struggle will persist. Of course, victory comes only through struggle.

Karia offers sincere thanks to all those who, in these most difficult times, contributed in various ways towards the final end product. Special thanks to Godfrey, who read and arranged for others to read the typescript, and to Ros and Mel for typesetting the book.

Buzz Johnson
Karia Press

Acknowledgements

This book would have lost a lot of its force were it not for the consultations and interviews with persons who were in fact a part of this saga.

I wish to record therefore, my gratitude to Mr Ivor Cummings, Assistant Welfare Officer at the Colonial Office at the time, whose opinions were of much help to me in formulating a corrective view of the situation as it really was;

to Mr Thomas Lambey, an ex-forester at the Golspie Camp, whose opinion and experiences were of much use to a 'balanced' view of relations with the local community in the North West of Scotland;

to Mr Ambrose Thomas, who was at the East Linton Camp and was present on the sad occassion of the misadventure—death by suffocation—of a young forester;

to Mr Carlton Fairweather, who was the person to have the interview with the Consul General at Camp Harahan, New Orleans in 1942, where the men of the Second Contingent had been under semi-confinement while in transit to the U.K.;

to Mr Norman Young, now chemist in Belize and whose valuable help in reminiscences of the camp life also helped to give additional force to the argument presented in this book.

To the innumerable others – including local Scots at: Kirkpatrick Fleming, Newcastle-on-Tyne and elsewhere whose observations helped in the final presentation of the narrative.

To all these persons I extend my unreserved sense of gratitude for their help.

Amos A. Ford

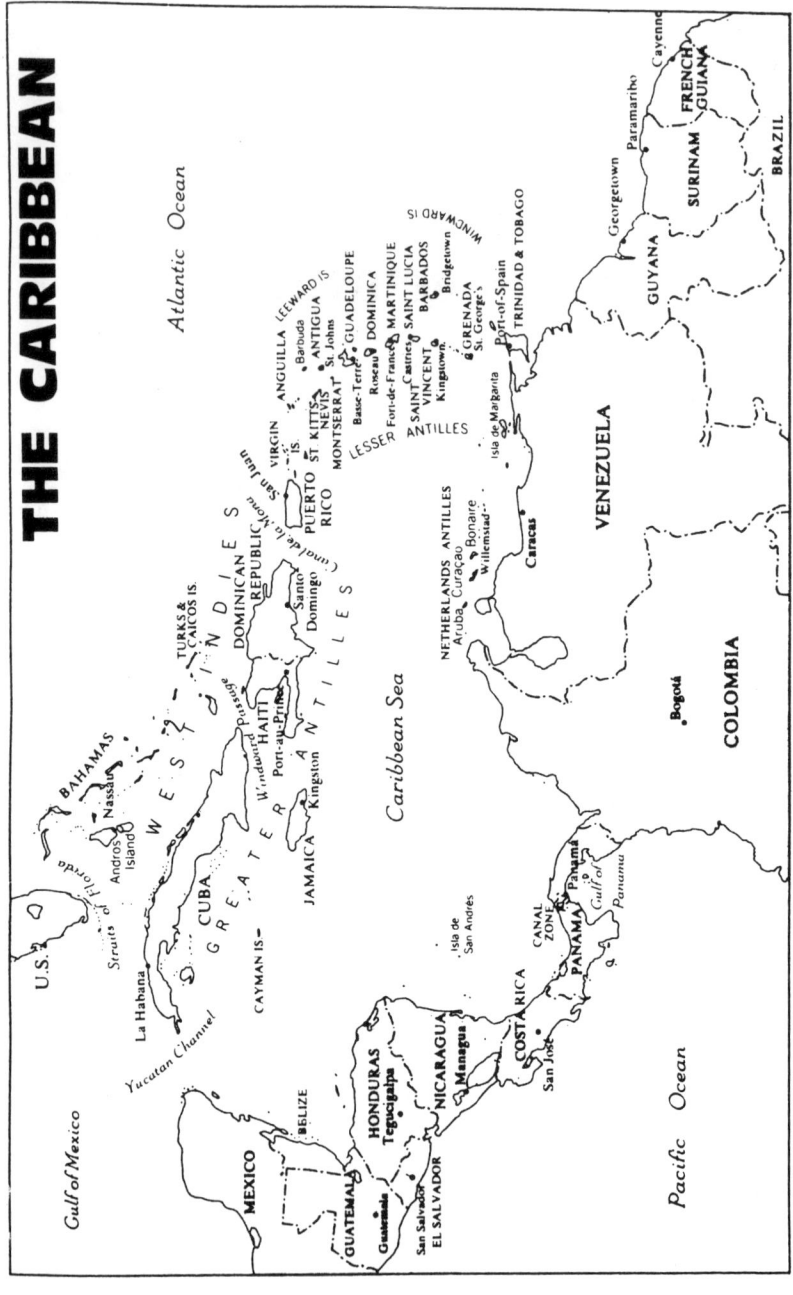

1 An Introduction to Belize in History

Belize, formerly British Honduras, is situated on the Central American main-land. It is bordered by the Yucatan region of Mexico to the north and north-west, by Guatemala on the south and south-west and on the east by the Bay of Honduras in the Caribbean sea. The country occupies an area of 8866 square miles, being 75 miles in width from the sea to the Guatemalan border in the west and 174 miles from the Rio Hondo in the north with the Mexican border to the River Sarstoon in the south, which is the southern border with Guatemala. The Belize River (full name) flows from the Guatemala border to the Caribbean sea to create Belize City at its mouth.

The coastal areas are swampy, being just a few feet above sea level, and the coastline is saturated with islets, referred to as cayes. As one moves inland, the terrain changes to flat, fertile areas in the northern sector with a more varied terrain of mountains, ridges, valleys, savannahs and forests in the west and south. These areas are well drained by the many rivers.

With its tropical climate the country is well known for the timber its forests were formerly endowed with. The population of 146,000 (1980 census) is concentrated mainly along the coast with about 33% living in Belize City.

Numerous ruins indicate that for hundreds of years Belize was heavily populated by the Mayan Indians, whose relatively advanced civilization reached its height between A.D. 300 and 900. Thereafter, for reasons not yet fully known, the civilization collapsed and many of the people migrated.

In 1502, Columbus sailed into and named the Bay of Honduras, but he did not actually visit the area later known as British Honduras.

The first recorded European settlement was established in 1638 by shipwrecked British sailors. This was later augumented by disbanded British soldiers and sailors after the capture of Jamaica from Spain in 1655. The settlement, whose main activity was logwood cutting (logwood was used in the past to produce dye), had a troubled history during the next 150 years. It was subject to numerous attacks from neighbouring Spanish settlements (Spain claimed sovereignty over the entire New World except for regions in South America assigned to Portugal).

It was only in 1763 that Spain in the Treaty of Paris allowed the British settlers to engage in the logwood industry. This was reaffirmed by the Treaty of Versailles in 1783 and the area of logwood concession was extended by the Convention of London in 1786. But Spanish attacks continued until a decisive victory was won by the settlers, with British Naval support, in the Battle of St. Georges Caye in 1798. After that, British control over the settlement gradually increased and in 1862 British Honduras was formally declared a British colony.

As the war between Europe for the American and Caribbean countries intensified during the 17th century, the Piracy Act by the British reached new heights. The Cayes in the Bay of Honduras were ideal hide-outs for such sea ambushes and very soon settlements sprang-up both on Cayes and the coastal areas of the mainland.

Settlers soon discovered the logwood much needed for its dye content, and lucrative trade developed with Britain. The first settlements were established at the mouth of the Belize river and a lobby for formal recognition of it by the British Government was pushed by trading interests.

From around the mid-17th century the British operated against the wishes of Spain. Numerous attacks were launched to destroy the settlements but destroyed towns were simply rebuilt and log-cutting and export intensified. At the same time, the lobby for the recognition of the settlement as a colony, which would also make the British Government responsible for defence, grew.

Between 1763 and 1862, the activities of log-cutters spread and many more settlements sprang up. These were formally recognised and agreed between Britain and Spain. The wood-cutters were licensed to work on sovereign Spanish territory.

As the economic importance of the trade grew with expansion into mahogany and other hardwood, felling and trading operations expanded and in 1862, Belize was declared a British crown colony.

From then onwards, the consolidation of the extensive forest holdings into the hands of absentee corporate owners became the norm. By 1875 one company, B.E.C. owned one-fifth of the land area of Belize, and virtually controlled the colony through wielding its timber interests.

The development of agriculture was also prevented by the timber and log-wood exploiters who saw such industries as competing against their unnecessary imports of food stuff. Thus, the extraction and export of forestry produce continued unabated without any diversification in the economy. This left the colony wide open to the economic and technological shifts in Europe and North America, and international price fluctuations due to increasing timber exploitation in other central, and South American, and African countries.

The special nature of the production of timber required a peculiar relationship between the workers and the European settlers. In the case of Belize, the institution of slavery took on a form peculiar to that country, but there were no essential differences in practice as it developed in Belize and other countries. This is further evidenced by the fact that the process of dehumanisation of slaves in Belize was no different to that in other countries.

African drumming, dancing and the practice of the merry-making of GUMBAY, said to be noisy, were all prohibited at pain of death. Every effort to remove the Africans from his/her heritage were invoked with the uttermost vigour. These savage practices of the Europeans were the means whereby it was intended that the continued supply of the cheap labour of the slaves would be maintained.

This common belief that there was no slavery in British Honduras was patently untrue. Some writers assert that, if it did exist, it was practiced with every regard and consideration for the slaves' better interests — that it was 'humane'. These fallacies must be refuted once and for all. Of course, there were those of slave decent who prefered to turn a blind eye to the truth as it is known, or to reject their own slave past for reasons better known to themselves.

Even a Superintendent of the period, one Colonel Arthur, was forced to retract an earlier statement that the slaves were treated with much compassion and to say: 'THE SLAVES ARE DEPRIVED OF ALL PROTECTION UNDER THE LAW'. Additionally, as late as 1919, an official of the colony was known to have reported back to London that: 'THE RIGHTS OF EVERY BLACKMAN IN THIS COLONY IS AS SEDULOUSLY GUARDED AS THAT OF THE RICHES OF WHITEMEN'.

This statement was made after a Commission of Enquiry was sent out to investigate the riot which followed the return of the soldiers from the First World War, dissatisfied with their treatment in

Mesopotamia (Egypt) and because of the shabby treatment meted out to them on their return in 1919. Discharged with no pay, the inordinate delay in meeting their just demands was met with the usual contemptuous disregard and warnings of police action if their disaffections were not discontinued at once.

Their experiences were not to be very different from what as slaves they might have expected. They revolted. Similarly, earlier in their history they had revolted in May 1773, because of the very harsh treatment they had been receiving. This riot too, was put down and with the utmost severity. A few rebel slaves were hanged. Desertions were not uncommmon and the only way or 'escape' route was either by the slaves buying their own freedom, by enlistment in the British West Indian Regiment, or by 'Manumission' where the slave-master released his slave more out of fear lest the former went to hell on death, than out of any real sense of justice and humanity for the slave.

Indeed, there had been such masters who had compassion enough to release a slave, but this act must not blind anyone to the fact that such a master was extremely rare and was not much thought of by his peers. The myth, therefore, that slavery did not exist in British Honduras, should be treated with the disreagard it deserves.

One of the techniques invoked by the local merchants to discourage agricultural activity, was to select only the very best of the local produce and to leave the rest where they stood by the roadside. That surplus went to waste because the roads were bad and few and because unless the merchants would agree to take more of the crops of food-stuffs, it could not reach local markets.

When Kittermaster tried to secure a Colonial Development Grant to buy a Cuban Sugar Factory for the colony and thus reduce the import of sugar, he met with strong resistance. The legislature thought it 'a waste of money'! To this, the Governor had retorted with vehemence: 'your coolness towards these proposals is contrasted unfavourably in the local mind with your attitude last year, in urging on the Legislative Council the advisability of making a loan to Sir Samuel Hoare's Belize Estate and Produce Company'. (See CO/123/431/15th January, 1934, Kittermaster to Cunliffe-Lister.)

The expatriate businessmen had no intention of helping to create any kind of local industry which could interfere with their ability to continue exploiting the natural resources and masses of the colony. Kittermaster was worried because he noticed the continuing serious deterioration in living conditions of the poor. Governor Sir Alan Burns was in his turn to remark: 'This most backward and depressed colony'. The Belize streets were badly in need of repairs. There were narrow little open drains to let the rain water flow off the streets in which the children used to play at sailing boats with just a piece of board as the boat and a leaf as a sail. The ramshackled wooden houses that were falling down were a constant fire-risk; the water supply was very inadequate and the absence of a proper drainage system was a direct threat to health.

Disease was common and the mortality rate high, with dysentry, malaria and tuberculosis high on the list of 'causes of death'. There was indeed, a cause for alarm and fear of rebellion. Frustration with the local administration was to re-kindle old anti-colonial sentiments and also, at the same time, re-awaken anti-white feelings, both of which were seen as the real cause of their poverty.

By the end of the 1914-18 war, the cost of living had risen intolerably beyond the capacity of the poor to buy food. In July, 1919, the situation received wider notice when five-hundred disbanded soldiers who were on active service during the recent war in Mesopotamia, returned and rioted in protest of the high level of unemployment and cost of living.

In 1931, a hurricane wreaked havoc in the country, taking with it one thousand of Belize's capital city population of fifteen thousand. Added to this, the depression in the European and North American economies and the reduction in export of illegal liquor had a severe impact on the 'one-product' economy of the colony. (The illegal trade in liquor had been supressed by the repeal of the Prohibition Laws in 1933.)

It was in this economic climate that the Second World War caught the colony and its people.

The history of the life of British Honduras and of her labouring classes on the one hand was a chronicle of want and despair! On the other, those well-intentioned expatriates who had paid so much lip-service to democracy and fairplay, along with their Creole and Mestizo collaborators in the colony had been securing for themselves an excess in economic advantage over a 'circumscribed working class'. A class without power to defend itself. They, the business minority, exploited and exported their gains and profits to more secure havens abroad.

Disenfranchised, the Belizean masses were powerless against this army of parasites. Governors like Alan Burns in the early 1930s were as exceptional as they were themselves powerless in the face of this local business mafia!

When the American demand for British Honduras's Chicle and Mahogany contracted severly because of the latter's trade recession in the 1920s, some 30 to 40% of the British Honduras work force was thrown onto the streets looking for work.

The fate of the Belizean masses therefore, during the later colonial period was not much of an improvement on their slavery experience where their well-being was concerned.

Hence, the struggle for survival continued unabated during the twentieth century, as it had been during the earlier periods. Only the 'form' of practice and method of exploitation had changed. A new form of economic subjugation had been devised to meet the new would-be civilised pretentions that slavery was unacceptable. Now it had become a matter of keeping the population in perpetual want by denying it the chance to uplift itself by self-help. Farming was discouraged and the inordinate amount of goods imported was to make any industrial progress for the masses impossible.

2 The Call, Response and Preparations

As Hitler went about ranting and raving and setting the stage for what was to become his genocide war, mass unemployment was already a feature of national economic life in the capitalist countries. This painful reality plagued British Honduras through most of the 1920s and 30s and she thus faced the future with uncertainty and apprehension. Ironically, international conflict was to bring some relief to British Honduras by way of a few more jobs.

Amongst other pre-requisites for Great Britain to carry-out the war into which Hitler had drawn her, was the urgent need for timber. Before the war several countries contributed to the total tonnage of timber needed by British industries including the coal mines. From the Baltic States, Canada, France, Portugal and others came her much needed supply to supplement her own home-grown timber resources.

Her 1936 import of timber was over 4 million tons. From Finland came 2,500,000 tons; from Russia 660,00 tons; Poland 475,000 tons; and Canada 450,000 tons. This had, by 1940, been reduced to less than one quarter of that quantity. When Norway and France fell to Germany, the picture looked bleak indeed, and Britian had to turn to other suppliers for her needs.

In 1941, Sir Roy Robinson, chair of the Forestry Commission, held an interview with interested bodies to look at the picture and to formulate new guidelines to meet the situation created by the war. He intimated that at least 5.7 million tons were to be aimed at as a target for that year.

Britain embarked on a forestry recruitment drive to increase her own out-put of timber. 20 Canadian forestry companies were to be brought over to help in the drive but this figure was to be increased to 30 companies later. Even French foresters were contemplated though with the fall of France this was abandoned.

Commonwealth foresters began to pour in. From Canada, Australia, New Zealand and even prisoners-of-war, were to be used later as the war went on.

To complete the commonwealth picture, British Honduran foresters were recruited in 1941 and 1942. But the road for the British Honduras subjects was not to be as calm and easy as they might have expected. From the creation of the Unit and its transportation to the UK to their settling-in, all was to be accompanied by suffering, humiliation and in the end right up to their return to British Honduras, disillusionment with the venture.

As is usual, in times of national peril, Great Britain calls on her black colonial subjects in Africa, Asia, and the West Indies — as much as on her white subjects in other parts of the Commonwealth — to come to her aid. As usual, they come. They come in their thousands to do service, to be maimed, to suffer and to die! But they come. They come with alacrity charged with all the love and patriotism for England. So it was in Belize, (formerly British Honduras), which became independent on the 21st of September, 1981.

From the early spring of 1941, there began to flow anxious cables and telegrams between London and Belize, seeking to recruit in Belize a work force for operation in Scotland under the direction and authority of the Ministry of Supply. In Belize, officials were instructed to recruit some 500 workmen and their supervisors and have them ready to sail as soon as transport facilities could be arranged. It was urgently stressed that the men should reach the United Kingdom before the commencment of the Scottish winter in order that they may become, at least, partly climatised before they commenced work in the forest.

Under the instruction of the Assistant Under Secretary of State for the Colonies, Sir Alan Burns, a coded message was sent by Mr Rogers of the Colonial Office, to his Excellency, the Governor of British Honduras, at Government House, Belize City.

The message despatched on the 25th May, 1941 read:

> *Ministry of Supply are considering recruitment of a self-contained unit of about 500 skilled woodmen, as axemen and sawyers and would be glad to know whether suitable woodmen could be recruited from British Honduras. Unit would contain: Axemen, Sawyers, Blacksmiths, Cooks, Foremen and Specialists, etc. Only skilled workmen capable of felling a minimum of 2½ tons or 100 cubic feet of softwood a day would be accepted. If such men are available in British Honduras, Sir John Calder*

The Call, Response and Preparations   9

and the War Office would prefer that they come to England as civilian units on the same lines as the civilian forestry companies from Newfoundland. War Office do not want them as military units. The cost per head as civilians is only half that of military units and there could be the question of equipment, etc., which Colonel Lloyd says would be difficult. If they were not forthcoming as civilians the matter would have to be put before the War Council.

Officials in Whitehall were in doubt whether men in sufficient numbers would be available, though the men were only too eager to serve the 'national cause'. On matters of pay, another Whitehall official said on the 19th June, 1941:

It is important that we should have a clear understanding that the rates of pay are British rates. The wages proposed are arrived at by taking the basic time rate in the industry for adult home-labour of £3 per week. (Pay would be subject to British Income Tax)

But, from £3 per week, deductions were to be made for board and lodgings despite the fact that the Agreement stipulated 'free board and lodgings would be provided'. The men would sign an Agreement that they would serve for one year or for the duration of the war, whichever was the less. In the end, the terms were for 'three years or the duration of the war, whichever was the less'. They were to be repatriated at the expense of the Ministry of Supply and at their discretion.

On this question of pay, the British Government was particularly concerned not to antagonise local Scottish feelings that 'cheap coloured labour was being used', hence, the parity with local labour wage-rates. In connection with the question of general employment in the UK, on the 25th June, Mr Rogers told Mr Fitzgerald of the Ministry of Supply, Bristol, that the terms of agreement made with the woodmen could not very well restrict them from taking up other employment in the UK if they so desired as they were *British subjects*. However, he went on to say that in the said contract, it could be made clear *that such permission would not be granted.*

From the June of that year, as the pace quickened, the scene was to become one of restless, fidgety and uncertain movements on both sides of the Atlantic. Once it had been ascertained that the requisite number of woodmen was assured, it was the question of transport that was to be-devil and compound the already anxious situation. Five ships were to transport the men from Trinidad to the United Kingdom after being conveyed from British Honduras to Port of Spain, capital of Trinidad and Tobago, in one vessel. Accordingly, these vessels were to arrive in Trinidad as follows:

The S/S STRATHAIRD on 30th July 1941
S/S MOOLTAN on 2nd August 1941
S/S BERGENSFJORD on 2nd August 1941
S/S FRANCONIA on 4th August 1941
S/S SAMARIA on 9th August 1941
S/S ORBITA on 10th August 1941

The Captain of the S/S Strathaird received a cable instructing him to proceed to Belize, British Honduras, where his ship was to pick up the Foresters and thence proceed to Trinidad where the men would be divided between the above mentioned vessels.

In the meantime, in Belize, things had moved quickly. At the recruitment centre there were furtive activities as the men went in and out of the office at Gabourel Lane. They were buzzing like bees around a hive! Men could be seen everywhere; standing about, leaning against the wooden fence-palings that enclosed the Labour Office, or pacing up and down with the sense of urgency reminiscent of an expectant father awaiting news.

They had heard the Governor's clarion call and answered it. They were at the Government's disposal, ready to move at a moment's notice. They came down from the mahogany camps ready to move again instead of spending a few months with their families whom they had not seen for some six months while they had been in the Belize forests felling mahogany trees.

In this atmosphere of brisk human activity, one could feel the urgency and the determination reflected across the faces of the men as they gathered around the recruitment centre waiting to hear when the journey would begin. Little thought or consideration was being given by them to the perilous nature of the atlantic ocean infested, as it was, with German submarines and disguised enemy raiders which were attacking allied shipping.

They were determined to do their duty in defence of human freedom and dignity. They had never been beyond the confines of the Caribbean, nor had they, in the main, taken part in hostilities of any kind. The new war strategies and tactics that were in vogue, were as menacing as they were alien to them; but their determination was not to be swayed or diverted from the path they had chosen to follow.

This was the mood in Belize when it was known that Great Britain had declared war on Germany. They had waited patiently to be called and their response was as final as it was sanguine.

While the recruitment was taking place in Belize, the Colonial Office was getting on with those anxious cables and telegrams about the ships; trying to ascertain precisely where they were and how best to distribute the 500 plus men between them. Mr. Wood of the

Ministry of War Transport (M.W.T.) despatched a confidential letter to Mr. Rogers at the Colonial office. In it he said:

> With reference to your letter of the 16th July, and our subsequent conversations, I can confirm that we have made a signal to the C-in-C America and West Indies instructing him to send a transport to Belize to embark the 500 personnel of the British Honduras Forestry Unit and to return with them to Trinidad. There she will disembark 400 and proceed to U.K. herself with the remaining 100 on board ... The remaining 400 will be embarked at Trinidad in subsequent transport at the rate of 100 per ship.

So far so good. But things were far more complicated and all these arrangements were, nonetheless, to prove fruitless as well as confusing. The delays were causing apprehensions and much worry to those most closely associated with the venture of bringing the men over.

The next letter was from Mr. Rogers to Mr. Wood at the M.W.T. inter alia, he had this to say:

> Although we originally asked that this unit should for medical reasons arrive here by the first week in August, you told me yesterday that this was now impossible and you gave August 15th to 22nd as the dates between which the various sections of the Unit would arrive in this country. Although this is running it very fine from the medical point of view, we decided after consulting our medical advisor to accept this risk in view of the urgent need for the men. We have to consider this as the lesser of two evils.

At the same time, in connection with the expected arrival of the men in Trinidad, His Excellency the Governor of that Colony, Sir H. Young, had telegraphed to the Colonial office in London saying:

> Accommodation is not in fact available though we shall no doubt manage somehow. Internment camp and quarantine accommodation on Nelson Island are completely occupied with aliens and internees and passengers from the Winnipeg and Africa.

After the hectic and at times nervous telegraphic too-ing and fro-ing, the Governor of British Honduras received news of the imminent arrival of a ship to embark the men. A telegram from the Colonial Office, London, to British Honduras read:

> Understand S/S Strathaird will arrive Belize about 4th August to embark unit.

This was a sign of 'movement'. Besides being without money, or a pay-day to look forward to, the men were getting restless waiting to hear when they would sail. With their families dependent on them for food and the basic necessities of life, their situation was getting desperate. There were rumours, too, that the Colonial Office was considering abandoning the project altogether. Eventually, they were awarded 75 cents per day while they waited. Full pay of one dollar per day (B.H.) would become payable immediately on actual embarkation.

How far this all seems to me now since I had joined that queue at the recruitment centre to become one of those Lumberjacks who were to be torpedoed in the October of that year; I can hardly imagine! It's all like a dream! Sometimes, a bad one; at others, a very recent event charged with all the emotions and thoughts of a dangerous past! In retrospect, it is perhaps good for the soul. I don't know! All I do know is that it fills me with a strange sense of the past; of my own experiences and involvement in that tragic phase in human mischief and pain!

But something forces me to make an attempt in relating some if not all of that 'SAGA' wherein so many unlike myself, did not survive to tell their own story. Let us always keep them in the forefront of our minds and never forget that from them, was exacted the maximum price for that freedom in which they so ardently believed and were thus prepared to die! But mine is not to find or to explain the cause for the war of 1939-45! But rather to record as faithfully as I can, what in my mind's eye I saw or thought I saw and witnessed! To give the Belize people and the people of Britain, a glimpse of that sad experience in which so many perished; in which the desire to make our world a better place to live a price so high was exacted from so few!

3 The First Contingent

Farewell, Embarkation & Departure

At long last, the day actually arrived. On the 4th August 1941, the S/S Strathaird made her appearance. Like a huge mountain rising from the deep, she presented herself to the view of the almost transfixed on-lookers ashore who gazed at her both in wonderment and relief. They had waited patiently for this day. Now it had become a reality! There was no turning back, it was 'full steam ahead'. Gingerly, she coasted her way in between the many islands or 'Cayes' (as they are called locally) which shielded the British Honduran mainland from the ravages of the Atlantic beyond. What a sight she presented to the people, as she drew nearer and nearer dwarfing everything around her. She lowered anchor some three miles off the Belizean city port as there were no docking facilities to accommodate even vessels of 5000 tons, let alone a troop-carrier the size of this massive ship. From the shore, we gazed at her as she stood motionless in the blue waters of the Belizean deep: inside the reef. She did not bother to ride the waves that dashed furiously against her hull. As if with mild contempt or disdain, she stood with her bow pointing towards the deep beyond the reef. Perhaps she was glad for the rest. Perhaps just pointing aimlessly.

Over-head, seagulls, pelicans, frigate birds and others glided their welcome to her. Nearer the shore, the ever-hungry pelicans were dashing their bulks angrily against the water as they struck the sea to scoop up a beakful of small fishes they had observed from on high.

The Belizean harbour from a distance of three or more miles

presented the viewer with a scenery of matchless beauty. In front, there was the mainland with its perfect contour of the landscape and coastline. Behind, the hills of the cockscomb mountain rising some three thousand feet above sea level. Nearer, the colourful wooden houses with their corrugated red roofs and highly picturesque forms standing out in clear relief. The rosefronted gardens with their aroma, were in themselves sufficient to enchant any but the most cynical. Interspersed in all that scenic grandeur, were countless trees; mango trees, breadfruit trees, coconut trees, kinep trees, guava trees – the list goes on – and they help to grace the port's appearance.

While the troopship stood motionless at anchor in the harbour, hurried preparations were being made by the Belize Authorities at Fort George to give a farewell party for the men.

There, in a huge bondshed, those preparations were completed in record time and the day following the ship's arrival, the contingent, their families and friends gathered for the momentous occasion.

There was much eating and drinking to the strain of Belizean music. For a while it distracted from the seriousness of the steps contemplated by the men at such a time. I need hardly say that many tears were shed. The families and friends of those who had come down from the rural districts joined in the merry-making. Like the rest of the families, they too had come to say farewell to their loved-ones – men young and advanced in age.

As it turned out, many did not see their brothers, fathers, husbands and other relatives at the end of the war. A few died in battle while others were to die as a result of enemy action on land. Some died from other causes; others never returned. It was with mixed feelings that they participated in the superficial merry-making that went on through the night until early next morning.

The next day, after a brief and dramatic last farewell, we all prepared to board the waiting ship. All manner of craft were engaged in the task of transporting the members of the British Honduras Unit to the ship which stood almost motionless in the blue Belizean harbour. As on her arrival, so on that 6th day of August 1941, twenty-four hours later, she maintained her silent disregard for the waves that continued to pound against her bulk.

We were soon settled down on 'D' deck of the S/S Strathaird, and put up our hammocks in this temporary home of ours while we waited patiently for the vigorous throbbing of engines to announce the commencement of the journey. We were looking at our homeland, some for the last time.

Arrival and Stay in Trinidad

The journey from British Honduras to Port-of-Spain in Trinidad lasted some two days and nights. We reached Trinidad on 7th August, 1941, leaving Belize and all those happy memories behind. In the Port-of-Spain harbour, the hooting of ship's horns was a new experience for most of us. What a gathering of ships! Large and small, they all evinced one common feature; they had all come from, or were bound for distant lands having just dropped anchor after, perhaps, a rough crossing of the South Atlantic in U-boat infested waters.

The activity of the harbour was very interesting. Small craft were gliding up and down the harbour. Though somewhat doubtful about our own destiny, it was a new and bracing experience which we would not have missed for the world. As much as the Trinidadian people were to prove most welcoming and hospitable, so was the landscape pleasing to the eye.

Before long, a party of us were taken ashore to await forward transport. We did not know what was to become of those who stayed aboard. Thus, we parted company in many cases, never to see each other again during the three active years we were to spend in Scotland.

In Port-of-Spain, we were lodged in what later turned out to be part of an internment complex in the St James area of the city. But before we go on to hear of the exploits of those who were left behind in Port-of-Spain, we must first consider the fortunes of those who did not disembark with us.

The First Group to Scotland

In London, Mr. J.L. Keith and Mr. I.G. Cummings at the Colonial Office were to play a most decisive part in this 'sea-saga' before all the men had been got over safely to the UK. Because of the delay, concern for the men's health was reaching dramatic proportions. On arrival of the Orbita, it was discovered that she had accommodation for only a limited number of foresters, and the three other ships were unavailable. These were signs that arrangements to bring the Unit over began to collapse even before the S/S Strathaird reached Belize.

Mr. Rogers at the Colonial Office wrote to Mr. Wood at the Ministry of Sea Transport on the 2nd of August as follows:

The British Honduran Forestry Unit in Scotland

This is to confirm the arrangements which we made on the telephone yesterday about transport for this unit. You said that three out of five transports on which it was originally intended to bring the unit from Trinidad to this country could not for reasons of military policy, be detained in Trinidad to await the unit. There was therefore, available only the S/S Strathaird which is bringing the whole unit from British Honduras to Trinidad and one hundred from Trinidad to this country and another transport, which can bring a further one hundred to this country. I understand you estimate that these two ships should arrive here on approximately the 20th and 22nd August respectively. You said that it would be possible to bring the remaining three-hundreed odd members of the unit to this country from Trinidad on ships coming in convoy which should reach here by the end of August. In view of the medical risks involved by this late date of arrival I consulted our medical advisor and submitted the matter to higher authority after which I rang you up last night to confirm that we should be glad if you will make arrangements for the remainder of the unit to come in the convoy as you propose.

The proposal was for the S/S Strathaird and the S/S Orbita between them to share the 500 and odd men from Trinidad to the UK. To this, the Admiralty reacted quickly:
To C-in-C America and West Indies, (Repeated N.O.I.C. Trinidad) Most Secret 4th August 1941, from D. of S.T.

To avoid exceeding the numbers allowed in unescorted ships and delaying Mooltan and Bergensfjord, request 100 forestry unit be accommodated in Strathaird and 100 in Samaria for passage direct to UK. Admiralty agree that balance may be embarked in Orbita which should be routed to Halifax taking advantage of cover of U.S. coast. After Halifax, it is proposed that Orbita should be in convoy.

On 9th August, in spite of another telegram that same day, the Naval Officer in charge at Trinidad, was to tell the Director of Sea Transport and the C-in-C America and West Indies that 'No accommodation available Samaria, propose balance of approxiamtely 450 foresters be embarked Orbita.' How frustrating, how confusing.

When the Orbita did arrive, it was discovered that she had accommodation for only 280. In the end, the S/S Strathaird left with 114 and the S/S Orbita with 267, leaving 160 ashore in Trinidad. Thus the two ships bringing over the first batches of the foresters made their seperate ways for the United Kingdom. One travelled to the Canadian port of Halifax and the other via South Africa, to a port in Western Scotland.

On 23rd August 1941, the S/S Strathaird bringing the 114 men of the unit, docked at Greenock in the West of Scotland where the men were cordially received by Sir Alan Burns, Assistant Under Secretary of State for the Colonies in the company of several local Scottish dignitaries and Mr. I.G. Cummings, the Assistant Welfare Officer of the Colonial Office.

After a brief welcome, the men were immediately transported to their camp in East Linton. This was (the Traprian Law), where they would spend the next three years if all went well, felling the timber they had been brought over to produce. But their camp was – even after all the time spent in negotiating for their transport to the UK – in a sorry state of unreadiness and disarray.

Official reason given for failure to greet the men in a more convincing state of preparedness was blamed on the contractors, whom it was said had failed to keep to the scheduled time for completion. Whatever the truth, it was quite unsatisfactory as well as disappointing to men who had just experienced a rough crossing of the Atlantic in time of war.

This new discomfort, was to be added to their experience of waiting at Belize to know when they would sail and the problem of how to keep their families in the meantime.

The condition of the camp was so bad that the officials who had accompanied them from their port of disembarkation, had to sleep in the recreation hut while the men made do with tents in the cold night air of Scotland in late Autumn. Quite disconcerting an experience for men of the tropics! The dining-hall, toilet facilities, etc. were indeed, 'unfinished' and the men had to plough through ankle-deep mud to reach their temporary mess facilities, etc.

While the 'arrived' B.H.F.U. men were experiencing those discomfitures and deprevations, the other batch aboard the S/S Orbita, was ploughing a passage through the rough and treacherous Atlantic towards Halifax where they would await instructions to join the next convoy for the crossing to the United Kingdom.

Nothing more is known about the separate voyages of these two ships, save that they reached their destination safely in the end.

On the 19th September, or thereabout, the S/S Orbita docked at Liverpool in the West of England, and landed her passengers.

With the same speed as with the first batch, the second was conveyed to their camp – this time, in Dumfriesshire, (Kirkpatrick Fleming). There they began, almost at once, to fell the timber while, at the same time, trying to acclimatise themselves to the rigours of the Scottish winter in poorly prepared accommodation.

With them had travelled the second-in-command, Mr Philips, a very able Belizean.

The stay in Trinidad & Tobago

There were now 160 of the men left in Trinidad to bring over. We were lodged in accommodation intended for internees and aliens, but it was in reasonably good condition. The Governor of Trinidad had telegraphed to say 'accommodation not available though we shall have to manage somehow'.

The internment camp site was located in the St James' quarters of Port-of-Spain. It was very comfortable. The food was good and our freedom was not in anyway restricted. We could go about as we pleased. The only restriction was at nights when we had to be in by a certain time. We also had to identify ourselves to the sentry at the gate before gaining admission to the camp.

The month's stay in Trinidad, was to be a pleasant one with organised tours arranged for us by the Trinidadian authorities: to Tetron Bay and many other places of interests. At this resort, the Americans had a base of some sort. As one who shared in that Trinidadian experience, I recall vividly the incident when a US Navy truck No. 2734 was involved in an accident injuring a number of local peolple. Some days later, on 25th August, two RAF pilots were killed outright when their plane crashed on a mountain side.

In the day-time, we went wandering about the nearby villages and farther afield to a Point-a-Pierre and to San-Fernando, a very steep large-sized town beyond Point-a-Pierre.

Near Port-of-Spain, we went to watch horse races, and visited San Juan and other places. At night, we roamed the city looking for fun. Those more adventurous, would even go in search of the many prostitutes that plied the water front at Marine Square etc. Others, more restrained, went to the homes of newly made local friends. Indeed, it was a pleasant stay amongst a most hospitable people.

There were no blackouts and thus at nights the streets of Port-of-Spain were always brightly lit. The buildings on Tragarette Road and Marine Square, stood out in clear relief as the lights hit the commercial buildings and the few dwelling houses in between.

While we were still enjoying ourselves in Trinidad, the other two batches of the members of the unit were in the UK making their contribution to the war-effort. But from us too, a price was to be exacted unknowingly.

Our remaining days were spent in Port-of-Spain going here and there and everywhere seeking new experiences in that lovely country.

Then came the memorable day – The day of departure when we packed our bags ready for the move. The activities associated with 'departure' from any place, always takes on a somewhat ominous atmosphere until what is actually taking place sinks in. So it was at

The First Contingent 23

St James' Barracks as we prepared to vacate the compound, there began one burst of activity everywhere. People were walking quickly, others shouting, moving in and out of the various hutments and generally signalling the advent of imminent departure. We were not to know that our voyage across the Atlantic was going to prove an experience we could have done without. The wonders of Trinidad had come to an end.

While we were in Trinidad, I spent some sleepless nights also pondering over the future of mankind. As a boy, I could not readily understand why it was that men seemed so ready to kill one another! And to kill each other in the most formal manner with the service of a priest in the case of capital punishment. When I was younger, I recalled how I shuddered when I watched the Black flag unfurl after the legal execution by our Belizean authorities of a person convicted of murder.

I had speculated and pondered over the question of why 'GOD' who was supposed to be merciful yet, permitted this cold-blooded annihilation of another human being by the law. Could HE have stopped it if HE wished? All our training was that GOD WAS LOVE. That HE could prevent things from happening because 'HE WAS ALL POWERFUL' 'ALL SEEING' 'ALL MERCIFUL'. Why should HE not insist that we loved each other rather than fight amongst ourselves? 'HE made the birds of the air, the creatures that crept, the different colours of the rainbow as much as the different colours in HIS PEOPLE.' I have still not been able to cast off that spirit of inquiry.

Trinidad — The Embarkation Sept. 1941

Finally, we were carefully marshalled on that 11th day of September 1941, guided to the S/S Winnipeg and before long we were actually aboard this old tumble-down French merchant ship. It was clear to us, even without asking, that there had been 'hand to hand' fighting aboard the Winnipeg. Below deck there was blood everywhere – in some of the cabins, on the inner walls, everywhere. There were hundreds to thousands of loose cigarettes (of a horrible taste), called Uzul, or some such name, all around the place – on the floor, on the bunks, and even in boxes. Many of us took these cigarettes on deck in our pockets, but were soon to throw them away. They were awful. 'Captured' the vessel certainly was. What was the location and what were the circumstances of capture, we never knew. However, we settled down to life on this ship, not knowing what fate held in store for us. The Winnipeg weighed anchor and we were now on the first leg of a most perilous journey of some three and a half thousand nautical miles north from Trinidad.

As we glided out of the Trinidadian harbour, we watched in wonderment, the beauty of the sea enriched land masses, several of which seemed to have been placed strategically to protect the capital city-port of Trinidad – Port-of-Spain. The water was so blue! The gulls darted in and out, seeking a prey or on the lookout for what the ship's cook would throw overboard.

Before long, we had cleared the port and all those several beautiful islands. We were making for the deep. Beyond and to the eastern side of us, we could see that lovely 'Tetron Bay' where we had spent so much time bathing or on the beach. It was not many hours before land came into sight once more. We had completely left Trinidad behind us. This was the land mass of the small island (also former British colony) of Grenada where we anchored off the coast some little distance from land, and so could not see very much of the island. We left the following night.

4 The Western Atlantic: The Journey Continues

So, anchor had again been weighed and we were now truly heading for 'troubled waters' proper, the wide and dangerous North Atlantic. Out on the open sea, there is always very little to see so we can move much faster over those 14 to 15 days that we spent on board S/S Winnipeg on our northward bound course towards Halifax. Apart from several flying fishes that used to skim over the ocean's surface or those that flew so high that they landed on deck, there were only the whales to keep us company throughout. Their spouts fascinated the Belize passengers as they stood on deck and watched the 'antics' of the whales.

The ship was never in darkness while we were in the Southern Atlantic. In fact, on our fourth day out, there was a large ship travelling southwards, whilst we were northward-bound. One could see the lights coming from the port-holes as she steamed by. There was a brief exchange of acknowledgement by lights between the two ships.

On this very uneventful journey, there was nothing to report save the sea birds that seemed to follow the ship for days before deciding to return to land. Interesting, how these birds were able to fly out so far into the Atlantic and back to mainland at will. Every morning it was the same scene, sky, horizon and sea in all directions. The night sky has faces which, apart from sailors few may ever enjoy the privilege of seeing. The mystery that is the Heavens!

I stood silently awed, mesmerised and glorified at the revelation which the 'silence and darkness', interspersed by billions of stars and planets, had thrown open to my mind's eye. Not only was I seeing the magic and the eternal mystery of order, I was also witnessing the most tangible and irrefutable evidence which have existed, time without beginning and time without end. Eternity itself. One could lean on the side of the moving vessel at midnight and gaze in wonderment at it all. If the night was a moonless one, the mystery was intensified. Breathtaking! If trauma could in this context be permitted, I would have said traumatic. Too late now for that. Nonetheless, the conversations had their merits. They helped to keep our minds off the dreaded prospect of a torpedo. Even worse, of a German war plane attack on a vessel which had only one rear gun in her stern, as a means of self-defence and was travelling unescorted.

I was also personally worried because my younger brother had also been recruited for the war-effort. Although we had left Belize together, we had parted company in Trinidad and he had sailed across the Atlantic without escort in another ship, a vessel called the 'Orbita', to Canada. My brother was subsequently to be posted from Duns to Kirkpatrick later in 1942.

Again and again, I was thrown back on to myself — seeking anwers to the unanwerable. Will mankind ever learn to live in peace? I had read about the Romans and Greeks. And before them, the Egyptians and their contemporaries. In short, all I seemed to be able to recall was man's insatiable thirst for self-destructionn.

I had also by this time learnt something about Latin and Central American politics, because I had done a little roaming in those parts. These showed me how untrustworthy and flimsy are 'political agreements' with each party trying to convince the other that they are right. Agreements are to be broken at the drop of a hat when it suits the stronger party. Hence, all the forestry workers from Belize knew, was that we had embarked on a mission of assisting in a conflict which might only be a lull in international hostility and avarice, engendered by international duplicity, greed and arrant self-interest, regardless of the common good to humanity in general.

Such it is when men argue on subjects, the motives of which are to secure for themselves, all the advantages in a situation. This is the kind of talk about which one could literally hear the retorted echoes: cynics, cynics or pessimists. But it makes no difference, for it is the way of the world! Will it, can it ever change for the better?

In the circumstances, however, all those arguments and discourses that we were having aboard the S/S Winnipeg, were no more than the mere exercise of the lungs and the whiling away of time. We knew that much! But as I said earlier, there was so much time to while away. It was either that or we were gambling at cards and dice, or passing away the time asleep.

But there was to be some diversion from all this uneventful, tardy and dull day-to-day life at sea. So many men with nothing to do with the time on their hands. Even the potato protests which had been mounted on more than one occasion, could not break the monotony of sea and sky, day-in and day-out. The Master used to bellow to the protestors: 'If you don't want that, then there will be none at all tomorrow'. In truth, the potatoes were rotten, soggy and tainted to the palate. Uncooked ones had been held up for the Captain and First Officer to see that there was substance in our grievances. Very poor and sub-standard food we were being given most days. It was war, however, and even soldiers on battle-fields have complained about the bad or low standard of the food provided for them at times. It is said that 'an army marches on its stomach'. Sometimes, its stomach must be very weak! Perhaps there was nothing the Captain could do in the particular circumstances.

Storm

But excitement and apprehension was to come our way. Far away in the distant North Atlantic awaiting us, a force 10 storm. All dullness and boredom was to vanish without a trace. Around ten O'clock one morning all of a sudden, there was a burst of activity among the sailors. A menacing storm had been notified to the Bridge and the necessary precautions were being attended to by the deck-hands. Holds were being battened down, anchors and other moveable objects in the bow and aft were being firmly secured. Up to that point, nothing was said to us. This made it all the more confusing, if exciting, to us who knew nothing about emergency measures at sea. Speculations thickened. Were we preparing for a naval battle? If so, was it a fight between this partly helpless ship and the German Luftwaffe? Was it an approaching German warship? Was it a submarine that had been sighted on the radar or asdic beam or what? Of course, there was no cause for panic because the sailors were merely working fast. There were no signs of apprehension about their faces and so that in itself helped to reassure us that whatever it was, it was not all that bad. By the time they had finished with the deck of the S/S Winnipeg, one could see from bow to stern with little obstruction. The only thing which seemed ominous was that they had put up 'life-lines' all around the ship. This is a rope one held on to in trying to move from one part of the deck to another in bad weather conditions.

We continued our normal sauntering about the deck, going below into our bunks or generally just hanging around, speculating on the activities taking place. It was some ninety minutes later before we knew what was happening.

All along during the voyage from Grenada so far, the ocean had been relatively quite smooth. There began to appear before long, large and slightly choppy waves, but not yet mountainous. The wind was now distinctly fresher. White-headed waves were beginning to form. As the freshness of the wind intensified, so did the waves take on a more sinister and menacing look. 'What were we in for?' I mused. Thereafter, it was a minute by minute intensification of the overall weather conditions. So far, however, we had not been told to restrict ourselves to our cabins or anything of the kind. I suppose the conditions on deck would in themselves become more than mere passengers could take and so we would all trek below to the safety of the cabins and our bunks deep in the belly of the ship without instructions to do so. By late afternoon, we knew that we were in for some very special Atlantic treatment. We were in the vicinity of the Gulf of Maine – the Captain had passed that message down to us at least. Not long afterwards, we all made for 'safer havens' than the deck afforded.

Afer that, it was only the heavy rolling of the ship which reminded us of the weather conditions prevailing outside. Before long, some had begun to be sea-sick. Since leaving the harbours of both Belize and Port-of-Spain, none of us had been sea-sick. I suppose the gentler and less frequent waves did not disturb our metabolism enough to upset the stomach. But now, more and more men were learning the lesson of what the Atlantic in its 'angry moods' could be, or look like.

We were to undergo almost twenty four hours of such conditions before the wind and the waves relented and gave us a respite from one of the most frightening and unbelievable tossing and plunging sensations one could ever experience. Not much food was consumed during that rough passage. I am sure that, in silence, the Captain must have been saying to himself: 'That will keep them quiet for a while'. And he would have been so right.

After the bad weather was all over, it was nice to see the sky again and, although the waves were still quite high, they were certainly not such as to cause us to think the worst. The skies were clearing too. The clouds were low overhead but still moving fast. We enjoyed the fresh breeze blowing in our faces as we watched the waves go by one after the another. But no sooner had we come out of the storm safely, than we had begun an 'intensified' life-boat drill all over again.

Our passage had now taken us well up north, reaching out into the area on the fringe of the enemy 'U' boat patrol of the north-western Atlantic, and so it meant an intensified look-out for 'U' boats and enemy aircrafts. What could that single gun in the stern of the S/S Winnipeg have done had we been attacked? Perhaps Jerry knew the worthlessness of attacking such a vessel and therefore let her go her way, unmolested.

The end of the peril — first experience

It was with joy and excitement that we stood on the deck of the S/S Winnipeg, as the ship steamed between the island, drawing nearer to the port of Halifax. Now at half speed, she was making her way painstakingly among buoys and the lighthouse in the distance. Huge water balloons, like white drums, were bobbing up and down on the surface of the channel.

The excitement had built up from the time the storm had abated and we had seen friendly Canadian aircraft coming to welcome and escort us into port. We did have some kind of air-cover once, while we were further along the coast of Maine.

Inexperienced as we were, we did not know one stretch of coast from another when it came into view, unless some sailor happened to volunteer the information, showing off his superior knowledge of the area. The cause for the excitement was two-fold. First, there was an end to fourteen days at sea. Secondly, there was this sense of security – of safety. We were near land and people.

All around us life buzzed with activity. There was activity overhead, with the patrolling planes. Tug boats steamed up and down the narrow channel as slowly but steadily we approached the port and her huge dock – more an overhead bondshed than a dock. Once the S/S Winnipeg had been docked alongside this building, it was difficult for us to tell whether we were still aboard the ship or on dry land. The structure was so arranged, that it had compartments like a house built over water. From now on, we would sleep and eat in this strange, fascinating building by the dockside. It was from this vantage point that we were to pay our few and brief visits to the city Port of Halifax.

It was quite an experience – especially for a new-comer – to walk up Barrington Street, where all the cars (like those in San Fernando, Trinidad) had to park with their wheels turned well into the kerbside, to prevent them running uncontrolled down the steep narrow streets far below.

Halifax, as I recall it, is like Newcastle-on-Tyne, a darkish grey atmosphere, and a foggy, penetrating coldness. Not very gay for a city her size. I suppose the only way one could have assessed the lack of gaiety, or otherwise of the city would have been to explore her cafes, ice-cream parlours and places of entertainment and to walk around the place. We, however, didn't have the time and therefore we only got a quick impression of the city.

We saw very little, if any, indoor life there. We were impressed, everywhere we looked right around the bay. The people were nice and welcoming, ready to put one at one's ease whenever they could. It was also for us members of the B.H.F.U., our first sight of a marching-playing-band of the Scottish Highlanders, with their picturesque tartan kilts and shining buckles, the frills on the bagpipes and the twirling of the drummer's two sticks. We had never seen anything like it before. No detachment from this famous Scottish regiment had ever visited Belize and it was only by going abroad that we had the privilege of seeing them. We used to watch them march with great dignity and precision, flaunting their Scottishness and cultural tradition before the onlookers. It was a treasured experience that I shall never forget – despite the fact that I have subsequently seen many of the Highland clans in their regalia, marching or dancing to their traditional music on their own home ground. The vibrancy of the music kept me swaying from side to side, urgently tapping my feet to the tunes of the bagpipe and the tempo of the drums.

Departure from Halifax — 22.9.41

But this was all too short a stop in Halifax. A couple of days and we were instructed to pack ready for embarkation. After some hustling and bustling, we vacated the accommodation provided for us by the quayside and lined up for inspection. An officer came forward and we were promptly marched from the quayside to board a waiting launch. This took us to the ship, which in turn was to take us across the Atlantic. I thought, we are bound for some shaky old vessel for the worst part of the journey – the U-boat infested North Atlantic. The very attempt to cross the Atlantic ocean seemed distinctly insane. Only a madman or a very brave man, would embark on such a venture.

Many are still alive today who could tell a tale of an Atlantic U-boat battle far more effectively than I can. All I will try to do is to set down my own indelible memories of war at sea; of the thunderous flashes as torpedoes hit a ship in the convoy and sent her to the bottom, or sent her keeling heavily to one side while she tried to keep up with the rest of the convoy, or failed to, and became a straggler.

We boarded our ship, the S/S Svend Foyn, and were directed to the area that was to become our temporary home. That is, of course, provided we were fortunate enough not to be the victim of a German surface-raider or, worse still, of the vicious torpedoes of a German U-boat. Our ship had a huge hole in her stern through which whales were winched aboard and sent down into the slaughter-chamber, where they would be turned into consummables to meet world demand. But now, her task was that of ferrying men and urgently needed war materials across the Atlantic. She was a very sturdy and defiant looking vessel, of around twenty thousand tons capacity.

It was the end of September 1941 and we were preparing for the crucial crossing of the North Atlantic. There were hootings from ships' horns, clanging of bells and all the noises of a busy harbour. Smoke from some of the coal burning vessels made it clear to anything flying above, that life below was on the move, down in that semi-circular basin whose only exit was a narrow channel into the open Atlantic.

Once we had been shown to our quarters and unloaded our luggage on our bunks, we returned on deck. We were glad to look at the view for the last time. There were trains coasting along on the edge of the harbour, which certainly provided ideal anchorage in bad weather. What this gathering of ships was for we could not tell – a grand assembly of battleships, cruisers, even a submarine, among the ordinary cargo ships that were to be seen everywhere. But we weren't kept guessing for long. The ships around us were moving, slowly, but inexorably towards the mouth of the basin. We were sailing. Although it would take some time before we had all cleared the basin and were out in the open sea. There was no turning back for any vessel, unless, of course, the unforseen happened – like a broken propeller shaft.

It was around 10am when the first signs of movement had begun. Two hours later the slow trickle had become an organised, steady stream. The protecting vessels must have moved out earlier. I did not observe them leaving. Two hours – and we could still see ships coming out of the basin, now well in the distance behind us. Our ship must have been in the vanguard, so that we too were well into the open Atlantic. By night fall, the land masses had all but disappeared, and in their place was the wide open ocean. Canadian Air Force planes overhead circled the convoy, now fully formed and moving at the same speed, though on a zig-zag course, as an evasive tactic against submarine attacks.

In the semi-darkness of the evening ships could be made out only by their silhouette against the sky-line. Travel from now on, was to be in silence. No lighting or smoking cigarettes, no use of a torch of any sort at any time while on deck. Above all, no noise. A German submarine could pick up the sound-waves miles away, or an aircraft could detect signs of life below them from a match lighting a cigarette. If we made their hunting any easier thereby, it stood to reason that we would be endangering not just our own ship, but the whole convoy.

In spite of these orders, there was always one blockhead who did the exact opposite and caused many an argument. It was not unknown for sailors to break this golden rule, upon which our very survival depended. The frailties of the human personality are surprising! Clearly, no-one would voluntarily wish to put their own life in jeopardy in this way. Was it just absent-mindedness? But the consequences could be so fatal. Then there was also the Clever-Charlie, who thought that a single match struck would hardly be sufficient to attract the enemy. He could be right, but he could also be wrong. Ours, as the saying goes, was not to reason why, but to do or die. How very apt.

As we travelled through the night, the skies were dark, except for the distant, twinkling stars and a waning moon. We stood on deck looking out at the waves as our ship ploughed forward, zig-zaging. One moment we were heading in one direction, the next, we had veered to starboard some fifteen degrees.

At night the ships would draw in closer to each other. But as soon as it was getting light, they spread out into flotilla formation for better escort protection. The Commodore and Vice-Commodore ships, along with the rest of the escort fleet, were always on the periphery of the convoy. At times, they moved in among the ships, searching out suspect intruders. Night gave enemy raiders a good chance to pick-off ships, particularly on the flank and at the rear.

Our cabins were very good. Being a whaler, whose crew must have had to spend months on end while on expeditions, her living quarters were relatively comfortable. The bunks were two-tiered, not too wide, and there were lockers in the cabins in which we were able to store our belongings. Of course, our life jackets were always hanging from our bunks, ready to be put on at a moment's notice. When we went about during the day, we had to carry them with us.

On deck, we were carrying about half a dozen partly dismantled aircraft. By their appearance, they were reconnaissance aircraft or light fighter planes. The bridge was well forward, and the other quarters – including our cabins were well astern. So that there was this huge space between bow and stern. This was the space occupied by the planes. Here and there on deck were metal circles, like manhole covers upon which the boys used to roll dice. Each day it was the same thing. Usually about four groups could be seen throwing dice on those manhole covers – relieving each other of their Belize dollars or the pound notes they had acquired when buying things from the ship's stores.

The Attack — U Boats Amidst

But this was all to come to an end. One bleak and misty cold October day, we had opted for staying indoors. What good fortune indeed! For had we followed the usual practice of being on deck with the lads at their dice-throwing games, we would all have been blown to smithereens! Without any warning we received one almighty blow to the port-side. A torpedo had landed smack amidships!

All hell broke loose! The ship began to keel over fast, the lights went out in our cabins and all over the ship; there was a scramble for the nearest exit. Life jackets were hurriedly put on. Most of us carried out this intricate manoeuvre while at the same time making for the first exit we could find. For myself, I was in double trouble. I had taken off my boots to rest my feet, while in the cabin. But now in the general panic and darkness, I could neither find the boots nor get into my life jacket fast enough. It was all movement on the stricken vessel, which seemed to be sinking fast! We believed we were going to end up in the icy water. Finally, we managed to reach the upper deck and ran for our respective life-boat stations. So far, I did not appreciate that I had not recovered my boots. It was extremely cold, but in such a predicament, the cold was the last sensation registering in my brain.

We were to spend many hours on deck, in northern ice-berg waters, with me in my stocking-feet, while the search for the U-boat went on. The warning whistle on other ships could be heard as well as that on our own. To our relief, the ship had ceased to keel over. It continued to list badly, at about twenty degrees, but was capable of going on slowly provided the engines could carry her along. It was fortunate that the torpedo had not hit the engine-room in the stern. As for the aircraft we were carrying on deck, we lost about two. Those that stood immediately where the torpedo had landed, which was amidship, leaving a hole in the side of the ship the size of a house. Everywhere it was wild activity. Escort vessels rushing here and there, dropping depth charges and emitting their doleful hooting-whistling sound as they went about protecting the main body of the convoy.

The submarine had half-surfaced after the depth charge explosions and our guns kept up the attack firing until at long last, and without sustaining any further damage ourselves, we sank the sub. A puff of whittish smoke went up, and down to the bottom of the Atlantic she went! Her crew abandoned ship, and we rescued the survivors. The deck-hands, our lads, everybody was shouting for joy! At the same time, there were demands for the prisoners to be handed over to the howling crew: 'Give us the b......s!' ... 'Give us the b......s!' But soon they were out of sight, captives on a ship they almost sank.

Clearly this was only one of several U-boats in the vicinity of the convoy. They had been trailing us for days, waiting for the right moment to strike. But though ours was over, other battles were still raging. Depth-charges could be seen exploding in the distance. it was day time and the ships were reasonably spaced out. We saw several ships being hit and go down after exploding. In some cases they went down stern first in the raging submarine attack on our forty-plus ships.

Submarine Tactics

The German method of attacking allied convoys relied on using U-boats in 'wolf-packs' of up to ten at a time, operating as a unit. In co-ordinated 'search out and destroy' tactic, they stalked the convoys. Admiral Donitz – the U-boat Commander-in-Chief, instructed his captains to report sightings but to take no further action. They were shadowing the prey, once found, while HQ in Germany informed other submarines in the area to converge on the convoy for a concerted attack. Once the U-boats had arrived on the scene, they were to position themselves in the path of the oncoming convoy, ready for attack when they were in the midst of their quarry.

This hunting in packs proved to be a very successful way of wreaking maximum damage and casualties on allied shipping. The tonnage of allied shipping sunk from the outbreak of war up to December 1941, was very high, but German losses in the same period were high too.

Although we were quite shaken by the torpedo incident, we were subsequently quite contented and well fed. There was ample food and the variety was impressive. To get to the galley each day, or to move anywhere about the ship, we had to hold onto a life-line along the side of the vessel because she was listing so badly. One of my compatriots and I used to go to lunch together each day. All the way to the galley we would be chatting. Now that the worst seemed to be behind us, except the rough weather, our conversation about the war in Europe was resumed, and we speculated like a couple of experts on what the Germans could be up to. We still believed that Great Britain had the largest and most powerful navy in the world, and would not be long in winning the battle of the Atlantic.

The young sailors, many of whom were Norwegians or Danes, around the age of 16, were very highly-spirited and gave us much amusement. Indeed, during the worst part of the battle with the U-boats and afterwards, during the storm, they were a source of comfort and encouragment to us. They seemed not to know fear or danger, and one or two had actually been torpedoed before, they told us.

We moved about the stricken ship as best we could, keeping out of the way of the sailors working. The shop was still open, selling cigarettes, chocolates, souvenirs, and stationery. We posted our letters on board and wondered how they would reach their destination. Mail was censored, and we had been told not to mention the ship's name or where we thought we were heading. As a result, we had to keep making apologies for being so vague. I was later told by my parents that parts of our letters were either blocked out or in some other way made illegible by the authorities.

We were sorry about this, but understood the necessity for it. 'Careless talk', they used to say, 'costs lives'.

Continued Threats

It was night before we were told to leave the life-boat stations, for after the sub had been despatched, one almighty storm blew up. Hurricane force no less. The captain ordered everyone to stay put by their life-boats. Soon one and then a second vessel came towards us, flashing their lights. They were rescue ships, one a korvette numbered K41, and the other a light frigate. But the battering we were taking from those massive atlantic waves was enough to remind us that we might have escaped one enemy but not the other — the cruel sea. As I stood aft on the ship, I had to look above me to see the oncoming waves. They were both regular and gigantic. One minute we were plunging right down into what might have been the belly of the ocean, the next, we were moving up and up as we strove to ride yet another mountainous wave in front of us. There was no time to be sick. We were too frightened to be bothered about such things as sea-sickness. Our main fear was that the ship would break in two because of the gaping hole in her side. At every plunge we took, the ship shook so violently, we could not be sure she would survive the shock.

Amid these frightening scenes we also had to contend with the intense cold of the North Atlantic. The icy wind penetrated our thick, warm Canadian overcoats, our clothes beneath, and right to our marrows. But the storm hazards and mountainous seas, though they troubled us immensely, were dwarfed by the calamitous situation in which we found ourselves on a ship that could break up at any minute. I suppose that for the crew it was bad enough. For us it was horrific. The end seemed very near. There were times when 'Abandon ship' can't have been far from the captain's lips. If the order had been given, it was virtually certain that not one of the passengers — including the writer — would have survived those icy, tempestuous seas, not even in life-boats.

Then, as the storm began to abate, we could see, in the distance scattered ice-bergs drifting dangerously about the ocean. At long last, however, we caught sight of the land mass of Iceland.

I said earlier that nations broke international agreements when it suited them. The submarine warfare raging round us on that October day in 1941, was an example of this. For Germany had undertaken to refrain from engaging in the kind of brutal and merciless U-boat warfare she had unleashed during the first World War. Under the London Submarine Protocol of 1936, it was forbidden to attack helpless merchantmen on the high seas, but in the early stages of the Second World War, Germany completely ignored that agreement, and her raiders mercilessly attacked and sank many allied merchant ships in a manner that was truly unforgiveable. In Winston Churchill's word in November 1939, 'Driven from the gun to the torpedo, and from the torpedo to the mine, U-boats have now reached the "Acme" of villany'. Once again, mutual interest and international law had been subordinated to military expedients.

These words echoed as one reflected on the disregard for human life as exemplified in such villainous behaviour. The senselessness and futility of war as a means of redressing international grievances do not seem to have come home to the people who wage it indiscriminately.

As we stood shaking on the deck of the Svend Foyn, watching the battle, we saw that the ships in the convoy were retaliating with their depth charges, while the escort vessels in their turn, raced off here and there in an attempt to catch up with the attacking U-boats and blast them out of the sea. But this was easier said than done, in spite of the fact that the Allied navies had by this time learned to counter the enemy's tactics. Depth-charges and ASDIC (Anti-Submarine Detection Investigation Committee), had made life for U-boat crews as much hell as their torpedos made it for the allied sailors and their ships.

One of the most infamous of German schemes of 'disguised attack' ever recorded was the sinking of an Egyptian merchantman named the Zam Zam. She was steaming in the South Atlantic when she was sighted by a German war vessel, the Atlantis.

Disguised as a friendly merchantman, and flying the British flag, the Atlantis crept up on the Zam Zam, and when she was within range of the German guns, the Atlantis hauled down her false colours, replaced them with her battle colours and opened fire. While the Zam Zam was in the middle of making friendly signals, and without knowing what hit her, she had been struck down. The survivors were taken aboard the Atlantis and eventually transferred to another German vessel so that the Atlantis could continue her deception and perfidy on the high seas.

Ships sailing alone, like the tumble-down old Winnipeg that took us to Halifax, had been lucky. The South Atlantic waters were no less treacherous or forbidding than the North Atlantic, and the Winnipeg had travelled unescorted with only a single gun in her stern.

The American Atlantic coast-line was as much a target for shiping as the British western coast-line. If it was not a U-boat stealthily attacking, it was a mine cleverly laid by a U-boat, blowing up some helpless merchantman. Had I regarded the South and Central Atlantic with the same dread that I did the North, I think I would have reached Nova Scotia a nervous wreck.

Daily Telegraph, 13th October, 1941
'Torpedoed Ship Hits Back'
A torpedoed Norwegian steamer has limped into port under her own steam with a thrilling story of a 'duel' with a U-boat in the Atlantic. The Nazi Commander evidently intending to finish the steamer by shellfire surfaced three miles astern. The first shot went over but after a second round the U-boat disappeared amid a dense colomn of smoke.
One of the gunners said he was confident that the U-boat had been sunk. 'This is the first time I had been in action', he said. 'We fired three shots altogether. I did not see what happened to the third because of the smoke'.
A broken finger was the only casualty aboard the steamer which carried 160 men from British Honduras travelling to England for forestry duty.

A resting place: Iceland October 1941

All this time we ploughed on towards Iceland, but it was a few hours yet before we were to find ourselves in the safety of that country's home-waters.

In much higher spirits, we watched as the Sven Foyd limped her way towards the Icelandic harbour. We stood on deck, watching the passing waves and the view that was gradually unfolding before our eyes, and we could see clearly the land formations ahead come closer and closer as the vessel, made her way towards relative safety. We were leaving the angry Atlantic behind and entering much calmer waters, green rather than blue-black with depth, and with waves that rolled gently rather than tumbled one after the other, smashing against the bow and sides of the ship. Finally we entered what appeared to be a wide Fjord with points of land jutting out here and there. Then at long last, the suspense was broken and our impatience to be back on dry land once more finally evaporated. We rounded a point and into view came a port. It was still a long way off, but we could make out the boats in the harbour, the smokestacks on the bigger ones, even the houses – our first sight of human life on dry land since Halifax.

As the ship prepared to anchor, we all made excitedly for our cabins. Up to that point we had not been told that we were going to land. We had merely taken it for granted that, in the condition of our ship, there was little else the Captain could do but disgorge at his passengers the first port of call. So in this frame of mind we prepared to go ashore. Now in the calmness of our new environment, we could better observe the vast damage that the ship had sustained. To get on to dry land, we had to walk over dozen of small craft, moored side by side at the quay. From there it was straight on to lorries and a three-mile drive along the Caledonia Road – Which we were told the Germans had built before the war.

We thundered along, and were soon in the camp where a large number of allied troops – especially Canadians and G.I.'s were already concentrated. They were a lively lot not badly behaved, just very mischievous. For instance, one day one of them had painted a brown horse, white. We enjoyed our stay and the fun of collective communal life among soldiers from far-off lands.

In October the Icelandic daylight is very short, I would say, a maximum of four hours. When we went out of doors in the morning the sun had not long since left the horizon, though it would be quite late, and it wasn't long before it would be again setting. For me it was another marvel in the heavens.

Everybody in the camp, was so jovial and friendly, we had nothing to do but amuse ourselves—anything we liked, so we played games or read, talked or slept until it was time to be off for the last leg of the journey to the West coast of Scotland.

Our accommodation was good and the food quite acceptable. We even visited the little cinema in Reykjavik, where one was shown to one's seat via a rather tricky series of 'curtained' passages while at the same time, one's ticket was torn at each of the various stages in the manoeuvre.

For a cold country, at that time of year, I was astonished to see how popular was the ice cream. In rather large cornet-like recepticles they were rather cheap I thought, in price.

The Final Leg to Scotland

Our brief stay over in Iceland of about four to five days, was at an end, and we were on the move again. The last leg of the journey had begun. Out via the Denmark Strait, we ploughed our passage into the North Eastern Atlantic between Iceland and Scotland. The S/S Bergensfjoird, was a fast slim-line troop ship, but she swayed from side to side as her engines pushed her through the rough seas.

There were several submarine or air-raid alarms during the voyage, which sent us scurrying for our life-boat stations – but the very narrow passage and the rough iron ladders that led up to the deck, from below, made movement very slow as we climbed one after another to the deck above and thus, to our respective life-boat station.

That was the only unpleasant experience of the short journey from Iceland to Scotland. We weathered the dangerous crossing without any significant incident except when the ship's siren gave the alarm. It created a new nervous excitement which we could have done without.

No sooner had the Icelandic snow-capped mountains began to disappear, or recede in the distance, than the several Outer Hebredian Islands began to make their appearance and so engendering in us, a new sense of safety or hope of reaching land once more.

The scene hightened our excitement as we realised that soon, we would be out of danger, at least from the submarines.

Soon we were gliding up the narrow channel towards the port of Greenock where, without any further ado, we were whisked off to our camp in Berwickshire. The blue-bird buses that took us to our camp in Duns, were comfortable and moved fast over the road as if though they were being chased or that they were taking part in a cross country race. In truth, they were trying to get about their business before they were indeed attacked by one of those sneak low-flying German night raiders that so often attacked the Berwick coast. The night journey took several hours and it was daylight when we did reach the camp.

The condition of the camp when we entered the yard was awful. Ankle-deep mud greeted us as we alighted from the buses. We had to wade through this to reach the huts. Clearly, the management had no idea of what its task was. Men had been seconded from their East Linton camp to make-ready the camp site and the huts, for our arrival, but from the time that it was known that the men would be arriving, one would have thought that the Ministry of Supply would have seen to the conditions of the camps in a more interested manner. There were no signs of sustained official interest in the matter – or indeed, in the welfare of the men generally.

By the end of October 1941, all three batches of the British Honduras Forestry contingent that sailed from the port of Belize, in August 1941, had been landed in the United Kingdom. They were, however, poorly provided for. The conditions of these three camps along with those of the north, will be described jointly later on.

5 The Second Forestry Contingent of 1942

In spite of the many problems which the authorities had experienced with the bringing over of the first Unit in 1941, British Honduras was again to be asked to provide a second Unit for Scotland. Accordingly, the Belize authorities began to seek those men who had sufficient forestry experience in Belize for this second contingent.

In February 1942 a letter arrived in British Honduras giving the Governor details and categories of the men required for the task by the Ministry of Supply. As usual, the stipulation was, that the men should reach the United Kingdom before the commencement of the Scottish winter so that they too, could become acclimatised before commencing work. It was well realised that the conditions that would confront them was vastly different and severely more trying on their constitution than the British Honduras' coolest period in winter, would permit them to anticipate.

Those painful procedures of 1941, were to be repeated with the identical delays and uncertainties which accompanied the earlier venture in 1941. Several months later and 341 men at the ready, the second contingent was on its way to Scotland. On the 1st of October 1942, they sailed for the United States on board the U.S. troopship S/S Mataroa and were landed at New Orleans three days later on October 4th. There it was said, because of accommodation difficulties, in New York, they were to remain until forward transport could be arranged for them.

The New Orleans Experience

But the men were to find themselves embroiled in a wrangle with the local U.S. army authorities. For some inexplicable reasons, the British authorities surrendered their sovereignty over the men and handed them over to the U.S. Army, who promptly put them into a military staging post "Harahan", some ten miles outside of New Orleans, and restricted them to the camp. Added to that, the British Honduras workers were made to work for four to five hours each day, much to their annoyance and disappointment with their own officials for handing them over in this way.

There was no likelihood that any of the men would abscond and remain in the U.S. It was well known, how eager they were to come to the U.K. and make their contribution to the war effort. They were quite unlikely to jeopardise their chances by misconduct of any kind. That too, was well known. Hence, it becomes even more difficult to comprehend the British officials' reasoning in handing the men over to an authority whose treatment of its own Black subjects was well known internationally. The same indignities and humiliations inflicted on Black U.S. citizens, were to be inflicted on the Hondurans.

They protested and from that was to ensue a wrangle with 'charges and counter-charges'. In reporting the incident to London, His Excellency, the Governor of British Honduras, Sir John Hunter, explained how sorry he was that the men should have been treated in this way. He stated that, on arrival, the men had been handed over to the U.S. military authorities and placed in the above-mentioned camp. Governor Hunter wrote:

> *The long and uncertain delay before the departure of the Unit from Belize and the many rumours that circulated regarding the reasons for it, understandably was a great strain upon its members. That so soon after their departure the men should have been subjected to a further delay, in what appears to be a state of semi-confinement, is most unfortunate and might easily in my opinion, have provoked discontent of a much more serious nature than that reported.*

Besides being confined to camp and made to work, the men were treated without the slightest respect or regard for their position as 'guests' in their country by the Americans. As we shall hear from the mouth of one of the men, their humiliation was complete. With his lengthy report, the Governor had sent a memorandum prepared by the British Consul-General at New Orleans, who said:

> Captain Perrier, one of the Army Officers at Camp Harahan, having reported a general deterioration in conduct on the part of the forest workers, as a result of which he had recently found it necessary to place one of these men in confinement (released next day on the petition of his companions). I visited the camp and had the Unit assembled in the hall and warned them that they were at present under the jurisdiction of the U.S. Army authorities who would not tolerate the continuance of acts of insubordination, insolence, refusal to work, etc. I made it clear that Captain Perrier and his officers had full authority to preserve order in the camp, and that men who refused to co-operate in keeping fit by performing the very reasonable amount of work called for (not more than 4 to 5 hours per day) would be liable to punishment.

This arrogant assumption by the Consul-General, and his manner of speaking to the men, added fuel to the fire and brought quick reaction from them. One told the writer:

> We were confined like prisoners and made to work and were guarded over by white soldiers. We had become unsure of our position and could not understand either, the treatment meted out to us, or why our own officials had handed us over to the Americans. We felt more like prisoners-of-war than as volunteers travelling to the United Kingdom to do war work.

Their dissatisfaction and grumblings, drew from the army authorities even stiffer handling and closer guarding over by the soldiers. They were regarded as rebellious and insolent children needing a much firmer hand from the authorities.

As a result of the unrest which their unpleasant conditions had brought about, the army authorities arranged a bus tour for them to New Orleans, accompanied by an army escort, through the city. 'We felt like exhibits rather than visitors being shown around the city', commented one forester, later.

To make matters worse, a few of the foresters waved and threw kisses to the white girls on the streets, who responded. This conduct was much resented by the American camp authorities who promptly returned them to base and gave them a good 'talking to' for their impertinence in waving and throwing kisses to white American womanhood. Naturally, this drew protests from the men. They had not intended to offend nor, it seemed, was offence taken by the girls in the street who had returned their friendly salutations in the same spirit. Because of their reaction to the official attitude, one of their 'leaders' was put in detention, though he was released the following day. The Consul-General went on to say that:

> One of the foresters representing the views of the whole Unit, asked for an interview to speak on behalf of his companions in reply to the

allegation made against them. With great politeness, he presented the grievances of his companions. He charged the Consul-General with 'neglect' and said that 'U.S. troops in Britain were not confined by the British Immigration Authorities and that therefore, he and his colleagues should be treated in the same way'. In reply I told him that I had no intention of interfering with, or assuming any responsibility for the legislation which the Immigration Authorities saw fit to enforce, and I added that in any case there was no similarity in the case of the American troops who are definitely stationed in Britain and not, like the forestry unit, a party in transit.

But the Consul-General was to go further in his memorandum to Whitehall and the Governor of British Honduras. He suggested that certain named 'members of the Unit are dangerous to the morale and discipline of the Unit and would be better out of it'.

In so far as this matter was concerned, it seemed that the normal protocol and diplomatic relations that exists between nations was abandoned and that the Americans were given a free hand in treating British subjects with the same inhuman disregard and contempt with which they treated their own Black citizens.

Neither the Colonial Office nor the Ministry of Supply seemed to have recalled that these men were not accustomed to being treated with the degree of racial discrimination and indignity to which Black U.S. citizens were subjected.

The question must be asked: Had these men been Australian foresters, would the British authorities have acted with the same sense of not wanting to be 'involved'? Was the fact that the men were in the United States 'in transit' as the Consul-General so readily explained, a reason for relinquishing British control over its subjects? The official files on this matter are so one-sided that an unenquiring researcher would be left with the distinct impression that the foresters from Belize were in fact a bunch of unruly and undisciplined children who wanted their own way irrespective of the need for some measure of security in times of war.

Indeed, the Hondurans had been most polite in all their dealings with the American authorities as was exemplified by the very statement of the Consul-General when he tells of how verbally restrained they were, in presenting their grievances to him on his visit to find out what had gone wrong.

Another of the ex-foresters told the writer that their main point of grievance was with the way the British Consul-General had carried out his investigation:

He never bothered to find out what was our side of the story. He simply listened to what the authorities had to say at the camp and from there, he went straight into lecturing us on 'obedience and good behaviour'. I told

> him that the way he was speaking to us was as if he thought we were little children unruly and in need of chastisement, and that there were two sides to every story and that we should have been heard before he launched into his lecturing us. He did not reply.

Having admonished the volunteer-foresters for their temerity in questioning the way they had been treated, the British Consul-General and his entourage, returned to New Orleans. No improvement was made in the living conditions of the men and they remained in that helpless position until they were finally removed from the camp.

The Consul-General made out his report to the Governor of British Honduras who in turn, sent a copy along with his own observations to London. The Rt. Hon. Viscount Cranborne, Secretary of State for the Colonies, received the reports but decided that there was nothing to be done about them. Thus, the men had no redress and there the matter ended, except, for the records which were to be left for posterity to show the men as 'uncooperative' and truculent in times of war.

A week later, the men were on a train bound for New York to embark a ship for the last leg of their voyage.

On 25th of November 1942, they were landed at a Western port in the U.K. Mr. Fitzgerald of the Ministry of Supply at Bristol wrote to Mr. Whitehorn at the Colonial Office to say:

> *I assume that you have heard direct from Cummings particulars regarding the arrival of the second contingent. This is just to confirm as follows: The number of men who left Belize, was 341, and they disembarked, 330 at Glasgow, 3 at Avonmouth on 25th and 27th respectively. These three were too ill to be landed at Belfast and remained on board the troopship as far as Avonmouth. Eight (8) were left at New Orleans as being too sick to travel.*
>
> *(see CO/323/1863/9351/1A/42)*

6 The Camps
The Northern Camps

After much tribulation including the humiliating experience at New Orleans, the second contingent of 333 men were landed leaving those 8 who were too sick to travel in the United States.

They were lodged as follows: 120, in Golspie, 100 at Lechmelm, 70 at Achnashellach and 60 at Kinlochewe. These figures of course, included their administration and camp managers, a number presumably drawn from the southern camps until such time as the second contingent's full complement had been brought together. Unlike the units in the Southern camps, the new arrivals found themselves much isolated from the local communities, in some cases the nearest town was some ten miles away and most of these were rather small villages and a few hamlets. The larger towns and cities being some 46 miles away. There were no transport and even if there were, the men could not leave their camps as they were in military restricted areas and out of bounds in so far as the locals were concerned. However, the camps were in the main, better furnished than those in the South if spartan in their accommodation. For recreation the men had to rely on their own initiative to a large extent, though before long there was some kind of social activities including visits from the 'ENSA' concert parties and others. At one camp, there was even some evening classes in various subjects and the men were enthusiastic participants. Most seemed anxious to improve their education if only to drive away the loneliness of their official position. The Ministry's main pre-occupation was with timber-felling. Human spiritual, cultural and even material comfort was not visibly part of its thinking.

The camp near the little village of Golspie had approximately 120 foresters and was one of the luckier camps in regard both to the men's work in the forest, which was virtually on their doorstep, and their welcomed use of the village's two public houses, the Sutherland Arms and the Ben Braggie Hotel.

Mr. Theo Lambey, one of the former foresters at Golspie, told the writer in an interview:

> The people were grand; the village was like our own. The people friendly and accommodating. In the public houses, we were treated like special guests. They were really good to us. Of course, most of the people were the old and not too suitable for military service, the local womenfolk, children and the uniformed soldiers with whom we got on well.

What a contrasting picture to that which the ministry tried to convey to the public. Clearly, it was just a matter of co-operation between the people, the men and the Ministry, their employer, to see that things went well between the newcomers and the locals. Fortunately, the locals were of the right attitude of mind and made it easier on the foresters.

> 'It was lonely', said Mr. Lambey, 'but we never minded that much because the huts were clean and sheltered, the food was not bad and above all, the camp manager was a good man'.

What a verdict compared to what those in the south were saying of the management of their camps, except at Kirkpatrick Fleming, where the manager was a coloured British Honduran himself and therefore, looked after the welfare of the men. The two most isolated camps were Achanalt (Achanashellach) and Kinlochewe, which were part of a military enclave or northern 'lookout' for the British forces guarding that part of Scotland etc.

It was partly because of this greater degree of friendliness of the local Scots, which so annoyed the Duke of Buccleuch, the big northern land owner, when he described the local people as 'too zealous' in their interpretation of his injunction to be friendly with the British Hondurans. 'The local women and girls had interpreted too widely the request to be kind with the foresters', he went on. Under the skin, people are all the same in relation to that common humanity which is part of the spiritual response natural to the whole human race irrespective of colour. Like Golspie, the local inhabitants of Duns in Berwickshire and Tranent in East Lothian, and similarly those in Kirkpatrick Fleming, were sensitive to the needs of men, both the young and the not so young, from far across the sea. People who had come to help remove the scourge of German racism and bigotry. For men who had only just arrived from a warm climate, those conditions were truly severe and testing on their constitution. In the end, several succumbed to the dramatic change in weather conditon, but they were perhaps affected more, by the complete lack of attention to their needs.

Many days it was impossible to take them to the forest to work. Conditions on the roads and indeed, the weather itself made it forbidding to do otherwise than to find work of whatever kind around the camp for them to do while the bad weather lasted. If they did not work because of the weather, there was no pay. In addition to this, the men's own unit productivity was hampered by some 80 or more of the British Hondurans being seconded to numbers 1 and 3 of the Australian company units to do menial tasks at their sawmill. The British Honduras Units were made up primarily of mahogany cutters, men accustomed to felling trees immesurably larger than anything that could be founmd in either Australia or Canada. They were a contingent in their own proven right, not the skivvies for the other forestry contingents. Much frustration was felt on this score, by the men who thought that the Ministry was using them as lackies to the white forestry companies. Besides this, the Australians did not treat the British Hondurans as equals. The result was that while they got on well with the New Zealanders they were very unhappy with their position at the Australian's camp.

The records show the British Honduran workers as 'expensive low producers' although no one-to-one comparison had ever been made of their output as against that of the other forestry units. Some of the British Honduran boys were also on loan to the Ministry's own home-grown production units, further reducing their own production out-put. It seemed that for the Hondurans, it never rained put it poured. Similarly, their medical attention left much to be desired. Their medical officer, Dr. Patterson, who was also their welfare officer was unsuitable for the post. But besides this failure as their doctor, he was never at the camps, instead he was more content with being in Edinburgh and only paying occasional visits to the camps. These two latter points were the recurring theme of officials at the Colonial Office against Dr. Patterson's continued appointment.

Between Dr. Patterson and Mr. Brunton, the camp manager at Duns, the management and control of the Unit was indeed pathetic and distressing. The camp yard was muddy and ill-attended. There were bits of logs strewn between huts and all over the place making it resemble a lumber yard.

Half sick men were going to the sick bay for attention and returning dissatisfied with the poor medical attention. For all ills, it was usually the same treatment: a pink pill. The clothings were inadequate to match the new weather conditions. Many wore their tropical underwear for want of more suitable winter vests etc. They had only one battle-dress. In this they went to work and also relaxed in the evenings as they had no additional clothing which they had been promised on their arrival in Scotland, but which was months in coming.

Disgruntlement and disappointment was beginning to make itself felt and absenteeism began to grow. The writer was stationed at Duns and knew only too well, what those conditions were like. However much one disagreed with the conduct of those less tolerant under the conditions they found themsevles (after as many grand promises) it must be conceded that the management's failure to meet its obligations, was sufficient to provoke that reaction. There was however only a handful of such men yet the ministry never failed to make it appear that it was the entire unit which was behaving in such truculent manner. This was far from the truth.

The huts at Duns, for example, had huge holes in parts of the floor-boards and walls and openings in the ceilings. But letting in the biting winter night air, was not the only thing that were to make life in the camps a misery. The furnishing was badly inadequate and provision for recreation strident by its absence. The huts had single cylindrical wood-burning stoves in the centres to warm a hut accommodating around 20 men each in a building. In it the men piled logs repeatedly to stem the cold outside. Sometimes the stoves burnt so fiercely that they emitted sparks and an inordinate quantity of smoke much to the annoyance of the local R.A.F. people resulting in a number of complaints.

If the men elected to stay in at nights, they huddled together for warmth, played cards or criticised the management for all the ills — real or imagined.

To work in the forest the men wore mittens in handling the logs, which had been stacked one upon another ready for the trucks when they came for a load. But the logs became ice-clad in winter and were thus painful to handle with bare hands. The mittens became threadbare and worn-out but the authorities were exceedingly slow in replacing them, hence, the men had to undergo the additional worry and pain of handling frozen logs in winter time. The forests at which the men worked too, were usually in the more exposed areas unlike those of the white forestry companies from Newfoundland, Canada and Australia.

With hindsight, it is now easy to see or at least partially understand the reasons partly why absenteeism had been on the increase. In the face of all the various discomfitures and official neglect, the men were called 'lazy'. In his letter to the Rt. Hon. Harold McMillan, His Grace the Duke of Buccleuch had written:

> *I was told that on their arrival, they were quite a decent well-behaved lot, though lazy at work and requiring a good deal of waking up to get anything out of them.*

In his reply to those observations, Harold McMillan said:

> *When the men first came they were, I think, not lazy but intolerably cold.* (CO/876/41 P.R.O. Kew.)

Their only compensation, was the eventual friendliness and co-operation of the local people which eased their discomfitures.

To digress for a while, I would like to remind the reader, that it was war-time, the services of every able-bodied man or woman was needed. I fail therefore, to understand the meaning behind the following injunction from the Ministry of Supply, sent by the Deputy Head of Home Grown Timber Production Department, Sir Samuel Steel-Strang, to Mr. Fitzgerald at Bristol. It read:

> *My own view is that the foreman or whatever name is given to the man in charge of each camp, should be a whiteman. I think this is most important as we must respect not only the feelings of the proprietors of the estates on which the men will be camped, but we must also consider the feelings of the people living in the surrounding villages and cottages. I should suggest that we might try to recruit the chief man in charge of each camp from ex-Indian officers or ex-tea or rubber planters — men who have been accustomed to handling coloured labour. It may, however, be possible to recruit such white men in British Honduras and, of course, this would be preferable as presumably such white men would be able to speak the language.*

I confess both confusion and astonishment at the language in view of the fact that British Honduras had men of local background and ability to carry out any and all the requirements of the operation of 'timber-felling and administration'.

Perhaps, later-on, the attitude adopted by the Duke of Buccluech will help us to understand more fully, the meaning and implication behind those words. For he exhibited a marked sense of racism and colour prejudice.

Death at Traprain Law Camp

But let us take a look at a tragic incident which took place at the East Linton camp on Christmas Eve 1941, resulting in the death of a rather young forester. It will add force to, and highlight the appalling management ineptitude that prevailed in the camps, especially at Duns and East Linton.

The people of British Honduras had sent over a quantity of rum for the mens' Christmas celebration that year. Each camp received its quota and it was of course, the duty of the management to see to its proper distribution among the men. In Kirkpatrick Fleming, the camp manager had divided his quota between the Christmas and New Year so as to reduce the quantity given to each man at any one time. Half a bottle at Christmas and half at the New Year. At East Linton on the other hand, Mr. Robertson, the C-in-C was not that circumspect in his distribution of the liquor to the men. It was alleged that some of the men were clamouring for the early distribution of the rum. Robertson's response was to order the whole quota to be handed over to them in one go. The equivalent of a bottle each. The order was carried out and by mid-afternoon, a large number of the men were seen on the road to be the worse for drink.

Later that afternoon, a number began to make their way on foot, in their drunken state to the nearby town a few miles away. As they staggered their way on, a passerby noticed that some (including the deceased) were much the worse for drink and advised their return to the camp. It was said that he accompanied them back to the camp.

On reaching the camps, it was alleged that some of those who stayed in camp, took the drunken man over to his hut and laid him on his bed, face down. On going over to the hut later that evening, it was discovered that he was dead.

A minor scandal ensued and a report was called for by the authorities at H.Q. The report said *inter alia:*

> The deceased on being brought back to the camp, was taken to sleep it off. He was placed face down on his bed and suffocated on his own vomit.

Whatever the truth of the matter, it said little for the management and much less for Mr. Robertson, who after all, was the Officer in Charge of the whole Unit. He had tried to dissociate himself from the incident by saying that he was not at the camp at the time. This in no way relieved him from his overall responsibility for what happened in the camps. His subordinates maintained that he was 'in the camp' at the time.

7 Conflict between Departments and Management

To understand the attitude of these 'bad hats' as some of the men were called, by the Ministry, one must go behind the scenes and take a look at the conditions that made those men behave as they did.

There were constant problems of administration between the Ministry and the Colonial Office which the latter was constantly trying to sort out in making life a little better for the men in the camps. The running of the camps in the South especially, were in the hands of the most incompetent of officers conceivable. On November 17th 1942, a meeting was held to consider a Report by the Director of Home-Grown Timber Production Department. Presiding over that meeting was Mr. Lananton, a senior officer from the ministry at Bristol. The subjects for discussion were: administration, including the question of absenteeism, police action and women in the camp and immoral relations with women outside the camp in circumstances giving rise to local scandal.

Earlier, a few 'undesirable' women had been ejected from the camp and barred from it. But it was not just the presence of those few 'loose' women which the Ministry wanted to keep away from the camp. It was also the visits by respectable families which it was the intention of the Ministry to try and suppress. Total separation of the two races was the ultimate objective of the authorities. The tactics did not work however, as there were no valid grounds for stopping what were clearly innocent visits of 'goodwill' by those respectable families from the villages or nearby towns.

Indeed, the meeting had sought to enlist the help of influential individuals locally in keeping in check this 'mixture of colour' which so annoyed the Duke and His friends.

On this latter subject, the Ministry said:

> It is considered that while the Ministry could regard itself as free from responsibility in such cases where Europeans only were concerned, it could not do so where coloured persons were concerned.

On the question of absenteeism, the Chairman explained that a number of the men had been convicted under the Essential Works Order and that the situation had improved. Mr. John L. Keith said in his report of December 1942:

> The general condition of these camps leaves much to be desired and there is no doubt that these unsatisfactory conditions are largely due to the administration of the camps. The situation is aggravated by the fact that the Manager of the Unit seems to have no administrative ability.

Reverting to Mr. Dunbar's report, Mr. Keith commenting on it, went on to point out that: 'even the compensation to which some of the men who were torpedoed, were entitled to, was being with-held.' At first the Ministry refused to pay the compensation on the grounds that they were not responsible for loss incurred as a result of enemy action. These personal effects, the Ministry maintained, should have been insured by the men against loss in the first place before leaving Belize. The officials also implied that the men were attempting to defraud the department by advancing inordinate claims of loss. The Ministry said that:

> Some of the men have made large claims. It can, I think be argued, that they brought an unreasonable amount of stuff with them and the Ministry cannot be expected to pay for all of it. Also as far as I can gather, the Ministry have no legal obligation to pay these claims and any payment will be 'exgratia'.

But British Honduras had been told officially, that 'compensation' would be paid for loss of any personal belonging due to enemy action during the voyage. In the end, the men were paid 25% of their claims and the authority waived payment by them of $15 advanced to them in British Honduras to buy clothing.

The foresters were badly and urgently in need of extra clothing. Especially warm winter underwear. Their flimsy tropical vests and underpants were no match for the Scottish winter. They needed waterproof capes. They also needed strong boots, and wellington boots to keep their feet dry in bad weather. But all these very necessary items continued to be lacking several months after the men's arrival. We shall hear what officials had to say.

Mr. Robertson, the Commander-in-Chief of the unit, Dr. Patterson and Mr. Brunton, the Duns Camp Manager, were the worst culprits in this chronicle of neglect. In one of his numerous minutes,

Conflict between Departments & Management 65

Mr. Rogers of the Colonial Office was to comment:

> Mr. Fitzgerald is rather inclined to sit back and wait for recommendations and reports to come to him from the officers in charge of the unit and from the Scottish branch of the Ministry of Supply. He is not unnaturally a little uneasy about efforts from here; to stir things up, constantly and make the point which is a quite logical and perfectly sound one; that the Ministry of Supply are entitled to expect the officers of the unit to represent their requirements themselves to the Ministry. The trouble is that Dr Patterson is a somewhat negative person whose spirit has been broken by years of service in the Treasury controlled atmosphere of British Honduras and while Robertson is good at controlling his men, he is not too forward in pressing recommendations for their welfare on the Ministry. In these circumstances Mr. Keith has the invidious task of trying to get things going by direct representations and by stirring up Mr. Robertson and Dr. Patterson to action.

On November 12th 1941, Mr Fitzgerald of the Ministry of Supply in Bristol had written to Mr. Rogers at the Colonial Office saying:

> Dear Rogers,
> I agree that at the moment, the affairs of the Unit are in a somewhat fluid condition and it is clear that we shall without delay, have to get down to a more regular method of running the Unit. We shall, of course, be always glad when members of the Colonial Office can find an opportunity of visiting the Units but, seeing that we have two such men as Robertson and Dr. Patterson, we feel that we shall have from within the department, very sound advice on all welfare matters.

The Ministry of Supply was not very pleased with the several visits which the Colonial Office was making to the camps. Mr. Keith the Welfare Officer at the Colonial Office, had written to Mr. Sanger at the Ministry of Supply (Home Grown Timber Production Department) at Edinburgh, expressing concern over some of the conditions which Keith's visit recently had brought to his notice. In a paragraph of his letter on 15th November Mr. Keith said to Mr. Sanger, inter alia:

> We were so impressed by the urgent need for warm underclothing for the men that on our return to the Colonial Office, Rogers got in touch with Fitzgerald.

On the question of the use of certain facilities, which were provided for service personnel, such as canteens and sleeping accommodation in the city, the men were at a disadvantage also. To gain access to such facilities it was necessary to prove one's identity by the production of some official symbol of authority enabling the bearer to use those facilities. In the case of the British Honduras Forestry Unit, this proof of identity was in the form of a 'badge' worn on blue berets which with the navy blue surge uniform comprised their only means of identification in public. Yet considerable time was to elapse, before the appropriate authorities would provide the unit with the badges.

Concerning the Duns camp manager, Mr. Brunton, Sir Alan Burns had made his position clear. He said that he could not take responsibility for the appointment of Mr. Brunton whom he said had been 'very unpopular with the men in British Honduras'. However, Brunton was appointed by the Ministry inspite of the reservations expressed by senior officers at the colonial office.

After a visit to the camp an official in a minute wrote: 'A sea of mud and very little had been done towards constructing paths across the morass'.

On the 29th April 1942, almost nine months after the men's arrival in the U.K. Mr. Keith wrote to Parkins as follows:

> *I think you should see the minutes of the 22 and 23 April, about visits of the welfare department to the British Honduras Unit. I do not understand Mr. Downie at all and I can see no case for limiting our visits — which in point of fact, have been all too infrequent. I visited the units in January and Mr. Cummings has visited it last week.*
>
> *I am afraid I cannot accept any arrangement whereby our visits are every few months. They should take place from time to time when we are fit and at the convenience of the Ministry. Let me say that there has never been any question of interference with the control of the Units — our visits have been ones involving advice and discussion and I think that they have been much appreciated by the men.*
>
> *You will remember that I felt aggrieved when it was alleged that I was not sufficiently concerned with the welfare of the Units and now, apparently it is thought that I am inclined to be too interfering. With regard to our past interventions I think that it can be said with truth that the pressure we have put on the Ministry to provide certain amenities and equipment for the Unit has been necessary and has avoided grave scandal as well as human discomfort.*
>
> *Again, the men themselves look to the Colonial Office as the representative of their government and knowing that we have an appreciation of colonial conditions and an understanding of the special hardships to which tropical people are exposed in this climate, they like to unburden themselves to us and to know that we are in consultation with their masters. Mr. Cummings' visits as well as that of Mr. Dunbar, the journalist, as well as an official of the colonial office are immensely appreciated and can only do good.*
>
> *Moreover, the Ministry has no expert knowledge on welfare matters at their disposal in Scotland and they are exposed to a great deal of criticism*

Conflict between Departments & Management 67

from the Ministry of Labour's officials as well as from private sources. They have every reason to welcome such advice as we can give them if only to protect themselves against attacks. But the attitude of the senior officials at 28, Drumsheugh Gardens has been consistently unhelpful and has lacked understanding.

Now, one of the objections to our visits is that they cause trouble to the officials concerned and take the men and their managers from their work. If this is so (I don't think it is really true) it is not our fault. We do not want important officials to accompany us, or cars to be put at our disposal, nor do we wish the men to be taken from their work. We take the local bus, we sleep in the camps, see the camps and men in the evenings, go with them to the village and to visit their friends or to the local pubs etc. and go on to the next camp by such means of transport as we can find. I cannot remember that either of us (Mr. Cummings or I) have ever requested special facilities, though sometimes they are thrust upon us.

Mr. Parkin's response is crisp and confirms the situation which gave rise to those observations. He says in his minute of April 30th:

I agree with Mr. Keith that the Ministry of Supply have no real grounds for complaining that our welfare people have been making unnecessary visits to this Forestry Unit.

I cannot help thinking that the feeling of the Ministry that the men are being 'over-visited', is largely due to the ridiculously combrous hierarchy and machinery of the Ministry of Supply itself. On any matter of even the slightest importance we were expected to write to Mr. Fitzgerald (at Bristol) who would then write to Sir. S. Steel-Strang (at Edinburgh) who would then pass on the matter, with his compliments, either to General Carrington or to Mr. Sangar, who in turn would then deal with Mr. Robertson (the manager from British Honduras), Mr. Keith has only just been able to break down this rather elaborate chain of communication. If as the Ministry now proposes and we hope they appoint a welfare officer, to look after these British Hondurans, and if Mr. Keith is allowed to correspond directly with the Welfare Officer, there ought to be no necessity for all this undue correspondence which so disturbs the hierarchy of the Ministry.

In any case, the back of the work has now been broken and the growing pains have been got over, so that there ought to be much less need for 'interference' by our Welfare Officer in future. (CO/876/41 minute of 30th April, 1942.)

On 14 April 1943, Mr. Keith of the Colonial Office drew up a report for the Ministry. It was addressed to Sir Charles Jeffries. It said:

This is a note drawn up in the Ministry of Supply for the information of the Minister about the British Honduras Forestry Unit. It contains a suggestion that the Unit might be sent back to British Honduras. I think this note avoids the real issue, which is that the Unit has never had firm and sympathetic leadership.

We have been pressing the Ministry to re-organise the administration of the Unit so as to provide this leadership, but we have not had any reply. 'In the meantime, the whole discipline of the camps depend on prosecution under the Essential Works Order'. This infers that discipline entirely depends on a system of penal sanction, whereas my contention is that discipline in the unit will only be satisfactory if there is proper leadership and this question of fines, penalties and so forth is quite a secondary matter.

Under firm leadership it will be possible to impose fines. The problem of the association between members of the Unit and women is serious but it can be exaggerated. There is no real evidence that the unit behaves in a worse way than the Newfoundlanders and the other 'foreigners' in Scotland, but they are coloured men and therefore their immoralities get more publicity and are more shocking to the susceptibilites of persons like the Duke of Buccleugh and his friends than would be the goings on of non-coloured persons. Here again the presence of women in the camps was very largely due to the fact that the Ministry of Supply did not provide satisfactory camp administration at Duns. As soon as the administration was tightened up, the situation improved and it is hardly fair to the men to suggest that unless penalties could be imposed on them, they will continue to behave in an immoral way, in the camps so far as this women question is concerned.

We have never had a comparative statement from the Ministry of Supply showing the value of the Unit in the matter of production, and it is not quite clear what the Ministry mean by 'being uneconomic'. The men may be expensive producers, but nevertheless from all one hears they are producing a valuable amount of timber. Their 1943 production should of course, be very much higher than the 1942 which was based on some 600 men only.

I suggest that we should ask the Ministry for a clear statement of production showing the unit as compared with other units.

But this suggestion was never taken up by the Ministry and the Unit's true contribution must therefore remain a mystery. Mr Keith continued:

I think we agree with the Ministry that the undesirables should be sent home and the sooner this is done the better. Owing to the slackness of the administration, of the Unit, quite a number of the men (a dozen or so) have already left the Unit and gone into employment. If the men who are to be repatraited insist on remaining in this country, I cannot resist them and all we can do is to try from the Colonial Office to keep in touch with them when they are in industry and at a later stage, consider ways of repatriating them after the war.

I would not agree that the men are "fundamentally lazy", but they are quite unaccustomed to regular day to day work (unemployment in British Honduras was always above 30%) and therefore needed special handling if good work is to be got out of them. I gather that in British Honduras they only work a few months of the year and spend the rest of the time in Belize. In Scotland they are expected to work a regular 5½ day-week, going to work at regular hours and returning in the evenings. They get stale, bored and restless. They will be encouraged if the Ministry go ahead with their proposals on pay and to improve leave conditions, and above all, they must have better leadership. (I think that the Unit is nearer 1,000 than 800) (see file CO/876/42) (letter from Mr. Keith to Sir C. Jeffries).

Regarding the provision of wet canteens in the camps, the outcome after much proscrastination, by the Ministry of Supply, was that they would not proceed with the proposal. Mr. Robertson wrote:

It is my considered opinion that the camps would be better without the sale of intoxicating liquor and that the question of instituting 'wet' canteen should be dropped.

Hence, inside their camps the men were not to have any form of relaxation. In trying to improve the welfare arrangements for the men, a Unit Welfare Officer had been suggested (CO/876/41). Mr. Keith was to comment:

I do not think that we can possibly agree that Mr. Robertson should be the Welfare Officer. We should do all we can to retain Mr. Robertson in 'general charge' of the men while they are over in this country but unfortunately, he is not of very high educational standard and not entirely acceptable to the Ministry of Supply. There was some suggestion when the question of getting rid of Dr. Patterson arose, that Mr. Robertson might go as well and as Mr. Rogers points out, his appointment as Welfare Officer would provide a solution to a different problem (meaning the embarassment of dismissing Robertson) (Mr. Robertson was a Scotsman seconded from the British Honduras Forestry Department at Belize to accompany the Unit as officer-in-charge).

Mr. Keith goes on:

Mr. Robertson is a good guardian of the general interest of his men, but he has not the initiative and imagination let alone the knowledge necessary for the job of Welfare Officer. Mr. Brunton and Dr Patterson were to be dismissed and returned to British Honduras in 1942, Mr. Robertson was as it were, to be demoted from officer in charge, and re-employed as 'Adviser', to the Ministry of Supply on matters affecting the Unit. One of the many criticisms against Mr. Robertson as that against

> Dr. Patterson, was, that he spent the greater part of his time in his comfortable accommodation at the Edinburgh office than with the men in the camps. Indeed, it would have been better to have employed a local man in each case to look after the administration and welfare of the camps than to have had either of these three men.

Since the arrival of the two separate contingents in 1941 and 1942 several visits had been made to the various camps by Mr. Keith, Mr. Cummings, his assistant welfare officer, Admiral Bromley, General Carrington and others. These had all expressed disquiet over the running of the camps. Yet the impression given by the Ministry about the men, their performance as lumberjacks, their relations with the local women-folk and their many complaints against the administration, was that the latter were not worth their 'keep'.

Indeed in parts of the official reports, the view was expressed that they were 'not satisfactory as woodmen' and should be 'got rid of' (see file CO/968/38/2, enquiry into the affairs of the Unit, January 1942, which was suggested by Mr. Rogers at the Colonial Office). As early as the 30th October 1941 Mr. Keith was already voicing his concern for the unit. He wrote:

> Mr. Stockwell the Accountant who was virtually in charge of the business side of the contingent told Mr. Cummings that the men are doing well, but he is dissatisfied with their living conditions. Mr. Cummings gathered that Mr. Stockwell, is quite likely to fall out with Mr. Sangar over this point and in our opinion, it would be a serious matter if he were put on to other work. (CO/968/38/2)

The outcome of the enquiry suggested by Mr. Rogers, was to reveal the true nature of matters as they stood at the camps. In a minute to Mr. Downie, Mr. Rogers said:

> This is a rather disturbing report which you should see. I think that we should wait Mr. Keith's visit to the camp next week before taking anything up with the Ministry of Supply. When we do, I would propose to write to Mr. Fitzgerald rather than to the branch at Edinburgh as though we have a responsibility for the welfare of these men. They are after all under the direction of the Ministry of Supply and we shall have to be careful as to the terms of our approach. (see CO/968/38/2 P.R.O.)

From the verbatim reports or quotations in this Book, and my remarks on them, it should be quite evident that there was a lot amiss in the administration of the British Honduras Forestry Unit from the outset.

In regard to their medical attention, there was no proper diagnosis or attention seriously paid to meet those conditions. Besides this lack of serious medical care, there were no trained medical staff and the doctor was very seldom in any of the camps. Colonial Office officials were always remarking on this point, but without much success.

As food ration coupons were restricted, the men were not in a position to improve on their meagre diet. Each man had a ration book which allowed him to purchase only certain items from the shops; eggs, fruits, etc., were essential in maintaining some kind of 'balanced' diet, but these were not available. Indeed there was little fruit for anyone.

With the poor canteen food and no means of supplementing it, the chances of keeping fit and healthy was a problem. It was to their credit therefore, when Reports adjudged them 'fit and well' in the circumstances. For it was stamina rather than official care which made them cope as well as they did. These were some of the conditions inter alia, which made the Colonial Office seem so 'meddlesome' as the Ministry of Supply was always complaining.

After midnight, the huts became 'FREEZERS' once the fires had gone out. For this reason, most of the men kept on their blue serge battle-dress tops and balaclava head wear in trying to keep warm in bed. When reveille was sounded by the bugler in the mornings, they were already awake. The very cold condition in the huts was unbearable and thus, the men were awake long before it was time to be up.

They were glad to get over to the canteen and get some warm food and hot tea to revive circulation of the blood and thus, generate some warmth in their almost frozen bodies. Hence, they were only too glad when reveille was sounded.

In regard to their travelling to work each mornings, they had another problem. The open cold trucks in which they huddled in trying to ward off the biting cold winds as the truck moved along the roads was indeed, forbidding! Sometimes, they boarded the trucks stricken with apprehension as they knew the severe weather conditons that awaited them on the way to the forest. But the Australians had 'covered trucks'. Perhaps it was because the latter were classified as military units. Whatever it was, the British Honduran boys paid the price.

8 Outside The Camps

Most of the Scottish communities in the vicinity of the foresters' camps, like those at Duns, East Linton, Kirkpatrick Fleming and as we saw earlier at Golspie, were very good with the men. Perhaps the Scots also felt a tinge of remorse for their latent colour-prejudice and wished to make amends. Right up to the men's departure in 1943 and 1944, relations between the foresters and the local Scottish communities remained strong and friendly. They used to visit the homes of several of the local people and even stay with them at weekends. The foresters had rationbooks for limited consumables from the local shops and were thus able not to impose on the goodness of their hosts. In larger cities and towns, friction did however arise over 'fraternisation' where the women folk were concerned. But this was no less so with the other personnel from abroad who had come over to serve the war effort. Of course, there was a stronger bias against the coloured men which somewhere in their copious documentation, was to be pointed out by the Colonial Office to the Ministry of Supply.

But while those few social battles raged, the fascist foe was doing his best unrelentingly, to reduce the capacity for self-defence by the brave defenders of the Kingdom. In the north, though the air-raids were not as intense as they were in other parts of the United Kingdom. Many weekends the men found themselves caught up in straftings and outright bombardment of cities and large towns where amunition and other urgently needed supplies were being manufactured.

At such moments, it was the bright flashes of the ANTI-AIRCRAFT guns (ACK ACK) as they tried to bring down an enemy aircraft which had been caught up in the brightness of the searchlight beams, which caught the forester's attention more than the actual bombing that was going on. The trails or pattern of lights left in the night-sky, resembled a gay fire-work display on festive occasions as the search lights scanned the darkness of the heavens above in seeking out to destroy the intruding aircrafts sent over by the Nazi to Bomb the cities and munition factories. In those situations, it was the blackout which though it did not stop Gerry from his evil task, was such a nuisance to the local community in their day to day life. For in trying to secure the factories and other places vital to the success of the war, cities and towns were 'blacked' out making movements in the dark a hazardous business for everyone. This was a major preoccupation in people's minds. The blackout did not just impose an inconvenience on the population, it also put life and limb at risk. The chances of being accidentally knocked down by a vehicle, was constantly present. The vehicles on the streets – especially army vehicles and convoys of army trucks jeeps and tanks on their way to some depot or other military establishment, moved fast along the streets and roads as much in day light as at nights in the blackout. Thus, the pedestrian was put constantly in mortal danger.

In 1942, there was a fatal accident in Kirkpatrick Fleming involving one of the British Honduras foresters and a local lady from that village. It was said that the lady was trying to cross the road in the semi-darkness of the evening when the forester noticed the lady's predicament and went to her assistance. Taking her by the hand they both proceeded to attempt to cross the road when, as if out of nowhere, came a vehicle with full fury, knocking them both to the ground. The man Mr. Ruben Law, was killed instantly, while the lady survived the night but died the next day. Today they lie buried side by side with three other of the foresters who died from natural causes. They are: Mr. C.A. Trapp, age 23 (died 17th June 1942); Mr. O. Leon, age 24 (died 17th July 1942); Mr. V. Baker, age unkown (died 27th April 1942); Mrs Jane Goldie (nee Anderson) age 57 (died 11th April 1942), accidental death and her companion Mr. Ruben Law, age 42 (died 10th April 1942).

The writer in pursuit of information went to meet people of that village to get their views on those war years. In the company of three locals, one from Gretna and two from Kirkpatrick Fleming itself. We visited the little cemetery to see the graves. As we stood there gazing at the five graves, there was nothing in our minds but how peaceful they all seemed. Companions in death holding hands as it were. Somehow, there was that rapt sense of peacefulness and joy enveloping their eternal silence. It was as if they were smiling on us as we stood paying our respects to fallen colleagues.

The visit brought back to my mind, a passage I had read

somewhere in the works of Mrs. Anne Killingrew in a panegyric to a friend in the 19th century. She wrote:

> No more shalt thou behold thy sister's face, thou hast had her last embrace.

So rest five warriors of that 'tragic experience in human mischief, pain and misery' of which I remarked at the beginning of this book.

But let us wander back through the streets of the cities and large towns where the boys of the Unit joined the sailors, soldiers, airmen and other serving personnel of the war to have fun and to fraternise with the women folk of these places. Edinburgh, Glasgow, Newcastle-on-Tyne, Tranent, East Linton, Dingwall, Inverness and countless other smaller towns and cities.

In the day time as at nights, columns of soldiers could be seen in their camouflaged vehicles as they drove through the city streets enroute to an army camp somewhere, or to a naval dockyard in readiness for embarkation. With their guns on their shoulders, or hung on their side, they marched briskly along to the cheers or at times, silence of the on-looking crowd lining the street.

Black or red beretted officers sat up in the cockpits of their tanks directing their passage through the city while the onlookers stared in wonderment and relief. Those tanks they knew, were intended as defence against enemy attacks in case of an invasion at home, or for active service in the innumerable theatres of war in Europe or Africa where our troops were engaged confronting the enemy.

The streams of convoys and marching soldiers, all gave the city the 'air' of a veritable battlefield. Of a beleaguered city bracing itself for the next surge of an enemy attack. But we knew also, that we could be killed by land-mines or sudden air attacks even in broad daylight, for the enemy was determined to inflict as much damage as it could on the cities and industrial areas in securing its aims of 'conquest by tyranny'.

In every way, the blackout imposed on the inhabitants were as much a menace as it was a firm reminder to us all that nothing was to be taken for granted in those darkened hours of war. Nonetheless, in that atmosphere of 'quiet' apprehension, everyone went about their business doing what had to be done irrespective.

It is only fair that the hospitality shown by the local Scots to the British Honduran boys should be mentioned in balancing this picture of 'LIFE IN SCOTLAND' for these lumberjacks. Their clothes were washed free of charge, even when payment in return were offered by the men, these were refused by the friendly Scottish families who had befriended them.

Several had the privelege of staying overnight at the homes of their new-found allies and friends. At Duns in Berwickshire, they were able to go with families to Whist Drives and participate in the fun and dancing afterwards. They were visited by several of the local families, husband and wife and in many cases, their daughters too would go with the mother or father to visit, usually on a Sunday.

The same situation prevailed in; TRANENT, EAST LINTON, KIRKPATRICK FLEMING and elsewhere visited by the men in search of recreation and some measure of distraction from the rather spartan conditions which the Ministry had made available for them in the camps. But as reward for their generosity towards the British Hondurans, those many families were to suffer the strongest resentment from their peers. The latter regarded them as traitors to their community and as such, ostracised them.

Such families as befriended the boys had very unpleasant names given to them. These were not just unpleasant, they were extremely offensive and uncharitable and included such words as 'DARKIE LOVERS', 'NIGGER LOVERS'. In the case of any woman 'respectable or otherwise', their particular appelation were 'PROSTITUTES'.

I suppose that it was these kind and generous Scottish families of whom the Duke of Buccleuch, that big landowner, had remarked:

The people in the neighbourhood were encouraged to be friendly to them and the girls have interpreted this rather widely.

In spite of the strong presence of racism among the locals, the foresters were nonetheless to experience a lot of genuine friendliness and comradeship at the hands of those who saw them as normal human beings and treated them as such.

There is little need to expand too widely or elaborately on the various kinds of treatment meted out to the men by the community at large. At times, the conditions were very discouraging. At others, quite the reverse.

9 Disbandment of the BHFU (1943)

From early 1943, rumours began to spread that the Ministry was about to send all the foresters back to British Honduras. 'There was enough timber' they said.

In seeking to disentangle itself from the mess which the Ministry had caused by mismangement and indifference, a meeting was held on the 8th September 1943, to discuss the Ministry's proposals for disbanding the Unit. The repatriation of some ninety-three men who were either sick, unruly and otherwise not of any further use to the Ministry had already taken place that year. Now however, the Ministry was claiming that there was sufficient timber with which to cope in meeting war needs. One colonial official at the meeting was to remark:

> It is quite out of the question to use the pretext of the prevalence of VD which is a preventable and curable disease in support of whole-sale repatriation.

After the interminable arguments and cryptic notes that had been passing between the two departments, the Forestry Unit was after all, to be disbanded. The effect of the earlier uncomfirmed rumours before the Ministry saw fit to let the men into the picture, was having a demoralizing effect on the contingent, both in the South and in the North.

The men depended on their weekly wages from which to continue sending home much needed assistance to their families. But since the Ministry had not hastened to bring the men up to date with events, the position was getting out of hand. Calmness in the face of uncertainty was being replaced with alarm and a sense of insecurity.

An official of the Colonial Office was to comment:

> *Some of the men are abandoning the camp without permission. It is important that they be told officially of the decision to disband the contingent altogether.*

The allegation that the men were 'expensive low-producers' too was showing itself to be quite untrue. In other quarters, the men's performance was being compared favourably with that of the other Commonwealth contingents (most of whom were highly mechanised units). As against the Ministry's own home-grown production units, the men were said to be better performers when at work.

The first contingent had only been in the United Kingdom for less than two years, and the second way up in the North West of Scotland, for less than a year. Because of those rumours, by the time the notices were posted up in the camps desertions had become common place. But it is only fair to say that the men were motivated by the desire to continue sending home much needed financial support for their families back in British Honduras. In some of the camps the men had organised themselves into associations and were writing to influential individuals enlisting their help in finding alternative work before the Unit should sail for British Honduras. Some wished to be trained as technicians, others as clerks, etc. Yet others made for merchant navy, or any munition factory that would have them. The situation had become frantic.

The Colonial Office too, was worried. It was afraid of the political repercussions which sending back such a large number of men to a colony plagued with mass unemployment would have. One officer at the Colonial Office had remarked:

> *The men had been frequently assured that they were doing a good and essential job of work in this country and have no doubt in many cases come over with a genuine desire to be of service to the war efforts. (CO/876/42)*

Another was to remark in similar vein:

> *I am informed by the Ministry of Supply that the policy in regard to the production of timber in this country, has for some time been under consideration and that having regard to the present supply position it has now been decided to reduce very considerably, the cutting of wood in the United Kingdom. In consequence, the Overseas Forestry Units, which were imported for this purpose have to a large extent become redundant.*

Significantly enough, other foresters were to be brought in to fill the gap left by the returning British Honduran contingents. The Ministry continued, in a letter to the Governor of British Honduras:

> The assistance given by the British Honduras Forestry Unit in this important branch of the war effort is greatly appreciated and their work has been most valuable. In the new condition that has arisen however, their retention cannot be justified and it is considered that they should be repatriated as soon as is reasonably possible, having in view particularly, the approach of winter.

In 1941, when the men were being so assiduously recruited, one Whitehall official had said exactly the opposite:

> We must accept the medical risk of late arrival in winter as the lesser of two evils. (CO/986/40)

Official Announcement

Later in 1943, officers from the Colonial Office and the Ministry of Supply visited the camps and in turn, spoke to the men whom they told the apparent reason for disbanding the Unit — those in the South as well as those in the North. Notices were posted up in the camps informing the men that those who wished to remain, would be found other jobs where possible, the others would be repatriated as soon as it became practicable.

At first, about half elected to go home and signed the form accordingly. Another quarter, said that they were undecided, while the rest elected to remain and continue their war effort.

In Belize, unemployment was about 30% most of the time, so that apart from the loss of a positive income, the men would return to certain unemployment adding gloom to local confusion. But as the reader will discover, finding jobs for those who elected to remain was an equally formidable task which Mr. Cummings, the Assistant Welfare Officer at the Colonial Office was to experience when he, in turn tried to obtain alternative employment, or tried to find accommodation for the men. Among the issues which Cummings was to find almost insoluble were new accomodation as well as the employment postings for the remaining foresters.

Institutionalised racism and colour-bar was strong among private as well as public figures. Earlier in this saga, in 1942, a *Daily Telegraph* article had reported:

> People from British Honduras are working in the forest of Scotland helping with the problem of post-war afforestation.

It continued:

> Announcing this in the House of Lords, today, the Duke of Devonshire, Under-Secretary to the India Office said that these men had been in

Scotland for some time and had begun to be acclimatised.

A note of warning was however, to be sounded by Lord Mottistone in his Lordship's usual conservative vein. He said:

Unless the Government abandon the propsals to send men from British Honduras to the Highlands, it would be landed in difficulties.

Mr Cumming's task was to prove harrowing to say the least. In trying to place the men, he had approached simultaneously the Royal Navy, the RAF, Rolls Royce and several other likely employers but with little success.

Through Admiral Bromley at the Ministry of Supply, General Carrington had made contact with the officer at the Navy Office responsible for recruitment, but Brigadier Cantrell, after much delay and procrastination rejected the approaches made to his office. In declining the services of the foresters as recruits for the navy the remarks were:

Apart from the quota difficulty with the Ministry of Labour, the Admiralty felt that coloured volunteers were rather an embarassment and difficult to place in this country.

To this view, Mr. Cummings had observed, 'I thought or was of the opinion that the colour bar had been removed from Navy Regulations'.

Mr. Ryder agreed and said that the men were not being kept out on grounds of colour. (See CO/876/6 minute dated 10th December, 1943.)

The approaches to Rolls Royce were to encounter a similar fate. After having agreed to allow a piece of its land to be used upon which to build a hut for the men (since families were reluctant to billet the men), Rolls Royce did a complete about-turn and withdrew the offer on discovery that the men were Black.

On this question of employing the men, Mr. Ryder at the Ministry of Aircraft Production, agreed to an interview with some of the foresters. However, they were rejected on the grounds that in two weeks time a couple of local factories were to close down and that the local workers at those plants would become available for the Rolls Royce jobs.

But the Manpower Board was to reject this view and observed that the work which the British Honduran workers were to do was unsuitable for the local labour that would be so released. Mr. Ryder was also doubtful whether the coloured workers would 'settle down'.

In the case of the RAF, the men were not to be accepted. One official said:

The British Honduran Forestry Unit in Scotland

> *We cannot expect the service departments to take 'strangers' from the colonies if it means that they have to forego taking recruits from this country.*

After much heartache and negotiation, some of the men were placed, variously with; the Scottish Motor Traction Company, in Edinburgh; with an oil-cake factory in Rochdale; with Messrs Turner Bross, also in Rochdale making airbrake lining and with the Edinburgh Railway Company.

Others found jobs by leaving the camp and making their own arrangements where the chances seemed likely, such as in the Merchant Marines, etc. But before we proceed any further towards concluding this sad story of neglect, there is one incident which so far has not been discussed but which is of paramount importance if the attitude of the Ministry of Supply is to be seen for what it really was. It concerns the fate of those ninety-three men repatriated in the August of 1943, via the United States of America.

10 The Ellis Island Experience (August 1943)

As noted earlier in 1943, the Ministry of Supply finally decided on the immediate repatriation of some ninety three men of the Unit, but as in all other areas of management (or mismanagement), the Ministry's bungling was to cause the men much unnecessary suffering at the hands of the United States Immigration Authorities. Somewhat indifferently, the Ministry had made arrangements with the US Consulate in Edinburgh for an outward visa for the men. In doing so, little regard was apparently had for 'landing papers' at the US port of disembarkation.

In consequence, on their arrival in New York on board the S/S Queen Elizabeth, the men were promptly detained as illegal immigrants and incarcerated on Ellis Island where they languished until all the proper documentation had been secured.

Records now released under the 'Thirty Years' rule, revealed that:

Arrangements were made with all departments concerned but it is now learnt that ninety three of the men are being held on Ellis Island. There is no question of their being criminals and it is requested that the matter be taken up either with Washington to secure their early release or with New York.

The question has to be asked: Why was an official party of travellers so indifferently catered for by the Ministry? Why, seeing that there was an officer in charge of the contingent travelling with it, did this not give the Americans reasons to be more circumspect in dealing with what at first sight may have appeared to them illegal entrants to the United States?

Was it because the men were Black, that made the difference in

82 The British Honduran Forestry Unit in Scotland

the way they were treated? These and others are all relevant points that need to be cleared up. The British Consul-General in New York had written to London saying that 'accomodation could not be found for the men, sick or otherwise, because of their colour'. The gravity of this incident and the anxiety which they were to cause, was manifested by their sending two of the foresters insane. The men had experienced the eagerness with which the Americans were ready to incarcerate them now on Ellis Island, as they had earlier treated them as prisoners-of-war in 1942 at Camp Harahan in New Orleans on their outward journey.

The British Consul-General at New York wrote requesting details by telegraph of the group transit visa said to have been issued. The Foreign Office in London replied on September 9th 1943 saying:

> We were informed that the American Consul in Edinburgh had recommended the issue of a group transit visa provided proper measures could be taken for the control and repatriation of the men on arrival and during passage through the United States. As visa was subsequently issued it was assumed that the foregoing arrangements had been made. It is now evident that this assumption was mistaken and that no arrangements for the control and repatriation had been made on the other side. We have also just learnt that the Ministry of War Transport cabled their representative warning him of the arrival of the men and adding 'understand Ministry of Supply making all arrangements for their stay in New York and onward passage'. This did not improve matters.

The Ministry's representative at New York denied any knowledge of that telegram. The Foreign Office in London sent an apologetic telegram to New York saying:

> We regret most sincerely that such an unfortunate slip-up should have occurred and that you should have had this troublesome and difficult job. If it is necessary to repatriate any more men, we propose to assure ourselves that everything is ready before embarkation.

When at long last on the 2nd of September, 1943, the men had been handed back to the British authorities, their condition of travel through the United States, Mexico and Guatemala, was to be their new worry on the last leg of the journey. The heat with unsuitable clothing for the tropics made it almost unbearable. Their condition was most pitiable!

In 1980. in Belize City, one of those early returning foresters said to the writer: 'These people are wicked. We never would have believed that it was possible for anyone to treat people like that'.

At the end of this tragic journey, Sir Godfrey Haggard, the Consul General in New York, sent the following telegram to London:

In view of the expense and very great inconvenience caused to the numerous parties involved, including the very understandable resentment felt by the men themselves at the lack of foresight and consideration shown in the method of handling their return, I trust that the strongest representation may be made to the department responsible (ie the Ministry of Supply), for the callous dumping of the men in New York without any adequate warning or provision for their transport. Recent demonstration in this country show the nervous tension that exist amongst the negroes and it is not difficult to imagine the unfavourable publicity which such a story might have given had it become known to certain sections of the American Press. (file: K12114/10372/245 on FO/369/2924)

11 Conclusion

And the persistently racist attitude of certain highly placed individuals in British society this side of the Atlantic was making matters worse than they really were. Bigotry coupled with latent prejudice continued to cloud the horizon and to make it appear that there was a great divide between the foresters and the local working people in Scotland. This was not true. Quite the reverse was in fact the case. Many of the foresters ended up being married to Scottish women, even when it was frowned upon by many in the society.

It was the attitude of certain officials whose susceptibilities made for 'bad' relations between the Black and the White communities of Scotland which helped to marr and exacerbate the situation.

An excellent example of the distortion can be gleaned from a correspondence between the Rt. Hon. Harold McMillan MP and His Grace the Duke of Buccleuch in 1942:

My Dear Harold
I listened with enjoyment to your talk on the wireless recently and thought at the time of writing to you about the British Honduras Woodmen who are working in this country. It is not my purpose to make any complaint against them, but I would like to ask if the Colonial Office or any other authority concerned with them has any policy about their association with White women?

I was told that on their arrival they were quite a decent and well-behaved lot, though lazy at work and requiring a good deal of waking up to get anything out of them. The people in the neighbourhood were encouraged to be friendly to them and the girls have interpreted this rather widely. As reports are coming in to me I made such enquiries as I could

Conclusion 85

from local residents and learned that there have been a number of marriages and births and much intercourse is allowed even in the camp itself.

I would have preferred absolutely definite evidence before writing to you. Personally, I dislike this mixture of colour and regret that it should be allowed with no discouragement. There are already sufficient births of 'foreign' extraction in the country without the additional complication of colour.

With the present travelling and petrol difficulties I am not often in the vicinity of the British Honduras camp but I believe and hope the civil population are now being quite kind and friendly to them. I do feel sorry for these people in a strange land so far and different from their own land and it is certainly my wish that they should be well treated and as happy as the circumstances permit.

At the same time I also feel that unsophisticated country girls should be discouraged from marrying these Black men from Equitorial America.

I hope the question can be dealt with judiciously as well as sympathetically.

Yours ever, signed Buccleugh

To this letter, Mr McMillan had replied in appropriate terms considering the Duke's prejudices. He wrote:

Dear Walter

I have just got your letter. I have been to each of the three camps myself and taken a good deal of interest in the men's welfare. I had heard some of the stories to which you refer, but only in a very unconfirmed way. When the men first came they were, I think, not lazy but intolerably cold. They arrived to the cold English winter from a climate which I understand is never less warm than the most highly heated hot-house in our old-fashioned gardens.

They therefore shivered and huddled themselves together and really did not begin to thaw out until the spring. About the specific point you raise, I am having a special enquiry made and will let you know the result.

Yours, signed Harold McMillan

The Duke and others of his views must really have been joyous when on the 27th of December 1943, four-hundred and twenty men of the forestry unit, with Mr. Robertson in charge, embarked and sailed for British Honduras. There remained in the United Kingdom more than half of the men, of whom a further 250 were to be repatriated between 1944 and 1948. The balance remained permanently and continued their contribution to the war effort.

Another highly placed official with views similar to those of the Duke, a member of Parliament, commented:

Watch carefully the social problems which might arise from the employment in this country of people from the tropics.

Right to the end, there were to be grumblings and complaints from those who had returned to British Honduras of 'bad faith' on the part of the Ministry of Supply. Several charging that they did not receive their pay for the journey back to British Honduras.

They landed in British Honduras in January 1944. The return of the 400 or more members of the Unit to British Honduras left a little over half still in the United Kingdom, to be accounted for. But the return of the men in 1944, was a sad affair. They had bravely faced the hazardous crossing of the Atlantic, with all its menace of enemy U-boats, the bombing while they were still in the UK and trouble in the United States. Now, they had come home to disappointment and despair. Quite unprepared, the British authorites 'seemed' to have had little idea of their responsibilities to the men.

Things had not changed from the experiences of the contingent in 1919. When those veterans of the First World War returned to British Honduras, they had to rebel to get anything done to meet their immediate needs. It was only the hastily summonded British warship that was called in to silence the returning soldiers in 1919 which prevented a more serious situation from developing.

Now in 1944, likewise, scant preparations had been made and the men were to return home to take up where they had left off – unemployed – and almost penniless.

Disgruntled and in low spirits, after much procrastination the men – or some of them – were given a piece of land in the fastness of the British Honduras bush, but with no means of developing the land. If any meaningful productive use was to be made of the land, official guidance and help was necessary. But this was not forthcoming.

Without money, the men could not work the land. They also needed some means of supporting their families while their crops came to fruition. They needed cash or credit in order that they may acquire the necessary farm implements, seedlings, and of course, the tools with which to work the land.

But none of these things were available. By the manner and style of their return, the men were being reminded that Belize, British Honduras was a land for those in power: For those who could fend for themselves, but certainly not for returning war-workers who had sacrificed their very chance of doing something for themselves at home. Nor to the memory of those who had fallen in battle.

Their disgruntlement was heightened by this insuperable barrier that stood between them and a chance of survival. The banks would not give them a loan unsecured. They could not get credit from the merchants because likewise, they could show no means of repaying that credit.

Many attempted to harness the land but failed in the end for want of support from the administration of the colony. The Banks and Merchants saw this as an 'inroad' on their preserves. For the effective production of local foodstuff, etc. was against what these exploiting forces in the country were prepared to witness. Hence, the reluctance to help the ex-foresters get on their feet by self-help projects in farming.

The Colonial Office had been much concerned with the repatriation of the men in the first place. They feared the consequences of sending back such a large batch of men to a land plagued with mass unemployment at the best of times. But perhaps Whitehall itself was reconciled with the knowledge in any case, that these men had been recruited from amongst the army of unemployed in the colony which made up a significant portion of the population. They were only being returned to their former condition.

Finding little or no work in British Honduras, many of the returned foresters sought an escape by immigrating to other countries, including the USA that had treated them so badly on their outward journey in 1942 and again, on their return to Belize in 1943 and 1944. Some made for Panama, Canada, and indeed, even to certain Central American countries. Others went to the United States via what was colloqually termed 'The Back Door' – that is, they went to some point in Mexico and from thence into the US undetected. Others made their way by 'stowing away' in banana boats. This was a very serious practice because if a stowaway became sealed off with the fruits in the hold of the ship under refrigerated conditions, he was almost certain to die of exposure to extreme cold.

Those who remained in the United Kingdom, became very widely dispersed throughout. Some found jobs in England, others in Wales, and a significant number remained in Scotland, working for the Scottish Motor Traction (SMT), ICI, the coal mines, with clothing manufacturers, on the railways and in several other jobs. In London, quite a number went to the various railway companies before nationalisation, where they remained until retirement.

Of the total that remained behind in 1944, a few hundred were repatriated between 1944 and 1948. Many took Scottish brides with them. Some of these women returned to the United Kingdom several years later, dissatisfied with life in British Honduras. In some instances, husbands, wives and children returned to live in the UK.

Appendix

Nominal Roll of Men Repatriated to British Honduras on 27th December 1943:
British Honduras Forestry Unit

1	78	ADOLPHUS, Charles George
2	351	AINIS, Issac
3	703	ANDERSON, Ernest Godfrey
4	710	APOLONIO, Vincente Francisco
5	640	ARANA, Eulallio Clan
6	896	ARZU, Albert Joseph
7	1055	ARZU, Matthew
8	460	ARZU, Odilio
9	461	AUGUSTINE, Benedict
10	1032	AVILEZ, George
11	213	AGUILAR, Pedro
12	2735	ALLAN, Ezekiel
13	2445	ALVAREZ, Roderick
14	2146	ALVARADO, Andres
15	2742	ARZU, Crispin
16	236	ALFRED, Edward
17	2611	ALLEN, Edgar
18	2269	ALONZO, Ernest
19	2455	ALVAREZ, Ernest
20	2446	ALVAREZ, Felix
21	2681	APOLONIO, Higinio
22	2180	ARGUELLES, Angel
23	2694	ARZU, Domingo
24	2450	AUSTIN, Charles
25	371	AINIS, Daniel
26	724	AMAYA, Melardo
27	458	ARZU, Vincente
28	725	ANDREWS, Hendral
29	832	AUGUST, Richard McKenzie
30	2499	ALMANDARES, Facundo
31		ANDREWS, Lincoln
32	2624	ANDREWS, George
33	2443	ARAGON, Pedro
34	2831	ARNOLD, Arthur
35	24	AGUET, Reuben
36	2732	ALVARADO, Pablo
37	2560	ANDREWS, Leopold R.
38	2663	AUGUSTINE, Prudencio
39	2643	AYUSO, Vicento
40	506	BARROW, Ralph David
41	1169	BAILEY, Conrad Gardield

42	722	BALDERAMOS, Maurice Alexander
43	558	BELGARA, Bartolo
44	1226	BENNET, Denbigh
45	650	BONILLO, Simon
46	154	BROASTER, William
47	1104	BROWN, Clarence
48	812	BROWN, Harold Lee
49	202	BURGESS, Oliver
50	579	BELL, Thomas
51	781	BELZONE, Rufus
52	467	BENGUCHE, Joseph
53	678	BREGAL, Catarino
54	285	BROOKS, Daniel
55	850	BROOKS, George
56	666	BROOKS, William Alexander
57	1014	BROWN, Augustus
58	628	BURGESS, Alan Samuel
59		
60		
61	2658	BARCELONA, Feliciano
62	2606	BARDALES, John
63	2804	BRADLEY, John
64	2161	BENITO, Stanley
65	2452	BENNET, Christopher
66	2376	BURGESS, George
67	2431	BAPTIST, Samuel
68	2265	BRADLEY, Gregory O.
69	651	BERNARDEZ, Anastacio
70	1030	BURNS, Frank
71	2591	BARNETT, Cyril
72	2561	BENNETT, Theophilus
73	2125	BRANNON, Hubert
74	2535	BROOKS, John
75	2772	BUCKLEY, Samuel
76	2811	CAIN, Clifford
77	2558	CLANCIO, Angel
78	2266	CARTER, Duncan
79	2548	CLARKE, Abraham
80	2634	CONNORQUIE, Joseph
81	2110	CUMMINGS, George
82	686	CALDERON, Philip Elijo
83	85	CARR, Alonzo Nicodemus
84	1084	CASTILLO, Antonio
85	463	CAYETANO, Edward Nelson
86	456	CAYETANO, Wilfred
87	693	CIEGO, Adosto
88	1123	COLON, Antonio
89	1101	CROWN, Selvin

90	662	CALIS, Emiliano
91	632	CASIMIRO, Peter
92	485	CHEVEZ, Bernard Augsto
93	1157	CHERRINGTON, Joshus Nathaniel
94	801	CLARE, Hildebrandt
95	2801	CARBALIO, Eluteris
96	2657	CARDINES, Braulic
97	2296	CARR, Oliver Hubert
98	2727	CASIMIRO, Conzales
99	2091	CHAPLIN, Walton
100	88	CARR, Cyril
101	447	COLON, Luther
102	317	CUTHKELVIN, Herman Clinton
103	998	CUTHKELVIN, Levi
104	2272	CLELAND, Patrick
105	2279	CHELL, Pedro
106	2457	CRAWFORD, Elphin
107	602	DOUGLAS, Abraham
108	2336	DAVIS, Malcolm
109	671	DIEGO, Ferero
110	2334	DOMINGQUES, Albert
111	2369	DUHANEY, Stephen
112	1131	EDWARDS, Stephen Eddie
113	1185	ELLIS, Ceno
114	884	ESCOBAR, Carlos
115	2696	ENRIQUEZ, Victor
116	171	ENCALADA, Dionisio
117	825	ESTRADA, William
118	2324	EVANS, Joseph
119	727	FLORES, Jose
120	1117	FLORES, Luciano Emanuel
121	660	FLORES, Sidney
122	180	FLOWERS, Arthur Wellington
123	396	FLOWERS, James Melvin
124	327	FRAZER, Edwin Robert
125	707	FLORES, Louis
126	688	FLORES, Justo
127	711	FLORES, Philip
128	1137	FLOWERS, Norman
129	563	FORTUNE, Samuel Augustus
130	2594	FLOWERS, Claude
131	2678	FLORES, Martin
132	2047	FLOWERS, Oswald
133	2494	FLOWERS, Hugh Donald
134	2780	FRAZER, Linford
135	121	GABB, Donald
136	737	GARBUTT, Aldrick
137	667	GARNETT, Joseph
138	477	GABOUREL, Sidney

139	390	GILL, Frederick
140	652	GOMEZ, Nasario
141	1244	GOMEZ, Ricardo
142	2403	GOMEZ, Victor
143	1161	GRANT, Samuel Theophilus
144	455	GUTTIERREZ, Enfernio
145	965	GARNETT, Herbert
146	492	GENTLE, Henry William
147	1242	GIDEON, Robert
148	648	GOTAI, Nicholas
149	795	GRAHAM, Rodwell Bicam Scott
150	858	GUERRERO, George Victor
151	2671	GABOUREL, Herman
152	2277	GOFF, Ludrick
153	2513	GUERRA, Diego
154	2429	GUY, Issac
155	2364	GALVEZ, William
156	1141	GARBUTT, Howard
157	2534	GARCIA, Thomas
158	2444	GENTLE, Samuel
159	2515	GOMEZ, Asterio
160	2379	GARBUTT, Harold
161	2466	GARNETT, Allan Herman
162	2333	GOMEZ, Leopold
163	2383	GONZALES, Andrew
164	2177	GONZALES, Crispin
165	2533	GREEN, Thomas
166	2737	GABRIEL, Thomas
167	2062	GONGUEZ, Marcelino
168	2294	GRIFFITH, James Noel
169	2691	GAYATANO, Isabel
170	2373	HAMILITON, Wilfred
171	337	HEMMANS, Dykan
172	704	HIGINIO, Percival Engique
173	952	HUMES, Ernest
174	680	HERNANDEZ, Cyril
175	880	HERNANDEZ, John Joseph
176	713	HERNANDEZ, Nathaniel Alexander
177	394	HERRERA, Egbert
178	759	HIGINIO, Edward
179	1102	HYDE, Ronald Calvin
180	2791	HILL, John
181	865	IFILL, Thomas
182	2703	JACKSON, Joseph
183	2680	JAMES, Henry
184	824	JAMES, Alfred
185	1086	JAMES, Henry
186	930	JULLITT, Elias
187	329	JEX, Roland Edmund

188	484	JONES, Edgar
189	2785	JONES, Ulric
190	2495	JOHNSTONE, William
191	2523	JONES, Reginald
192	91	KELLY, Christopher
193	2228	KELLY, Randolph
194	2209	KERR, Roderick
195	446	KERR, William Luther
196	1149	KING, Patrick
197	1175	LAMB, Hilton
198	466	LAMEY, Claudio Serapio
199	2153	LAURIANO, Henry
200	2622	LAMB, Haveland
201	2075	LAMBEY, Philip
202	684	LAMMEY, Frederick Alphus
203	673	LEWIS, Karl Allan
204	749	LEWIS, Seferino
205	718	LEWIS, Peter Maitland
206	595	LAW, Arthur Edwin
207	855	LOPEZ, Paul
208	2620	LECARDIO, Alexander
209	2838	LEMOTH, Nehemiah
210	2476	LEWIS, Charles
211	2549	LEWISH, Ernesto
212	2563	LEMOTH, Cardinal
213	2312	LOPEZ, Alejandro
214	2557	LOREDO, Matthew
215	–	LOPEZ, John
216	449	LOPEZ, Theodore
217	464	LOPEZ, Daniel
218	2367	LOCKE, Henry
219	2605	LOGAN, Lalman
220	631	LINO, Daniel Peter
221	644	LINO, Peter
222	890	LONGSWORTH, Edward Charles Dorrant
223	2327	LESLIE, Joseph
224	701	MACKENZIE, Joseph
225	2314	MATUTE, Pachico
226	2674	MOREIRA, Viginio
227	2370	MORGAN, Hannibal
228	2261	MORALES, Fermin
229	2787	MURILLO, Joseph
230	679	MARTINEZ, Andrew
231	501	MALCOLM, William
232	1126	MALIC, Amaro
233	969	MARIN, Maximilliano Albert
234	1026	MARIN, Philip
235	1253	MATUTE, Charles
236	489	MIDDLETON, Constantine

Appendix 93

237	28	MYVETT, Cecil Emanuel
238	809	McFADZEAN, Emanuel
239	848	MARCELO, Eidal
240	1051	MARTIN, John
241	854	MARTINEZ, Augustine
242	630	MARTINEZ, Alfonso
243	299	MARTINEZ, Charles
244	646	MARTINEZ, Stephen
245	699	MAXIMO, Marcus
246	753	MEJIA, Pablo
247	935	MILLER, Owen
248	733	MITCHELL, Leonard Cephus
249	1090	MONIMA, Luciano
250	426	MOORE, Burton
251	13	MOORE, John Ludevick
252	173	MORTIS, Rufua
253	811	MOSSIAH, Hugh Donald
254	894	McFARLANE, Charles Alfred
255	2520	MANZANERO, Paulino
256	2822	McKOY, Whitfield
257	2075	MORTIS, Harold
258	2512	MATUS, Cruz
259	2647	MILLER, James
260	2526	MARTINEZ, Enrique
261	2423	MOLINO, Enrique
262	2669	MONTES, John
263	2511	MASSIAH, Winston
264	2342	McGREGOR, George
265	2438	MENDOZA, Guillermo
266	2625	MONTES, Simeon
267	2366	MYVETT, Whitfield
268	2439	NAH, Andres
269	2291	NEAL, Dionicio
270	2573	NOVELLO, Emiliano
271	2685	NUNEZ, Chrysostom
272	433	NEAL, Allan Rowland
273	152	NEAL, Cecil
274	1113	NEAL, Cecil Alexander
275	495	NEAL, Fredrick
276	1050	NEAL, Oliver
277	401	NEAL, William
278	668	NEMBHARD, George Albert
279	1188	NORALES, John
280	691	NORALES, Leonidas
281	681	NOLBERTO, Florentino
282	2651	NOLBERTO, Lorenzo
283	867	NOBLE, Gilibaldo
284	876	NORALES, Robert
285	2645	OBANDO, Juan

286	2631	OLIVERA, Herman
287	2584	OLIVERA, Joseph
288	2603	OLIVERA, John
289	301	OROSCO, Bell
290	187	OTTLEY, Harold
291	2570	OZAETA, Antoni
292	2575	OZAETA, Eleno
293	682	PALACIO, George
294	846	PALACIO, Fulgencio
295	1193	PALACIO, Raymondo
296	761	PALACIO, Frank
297	649	PALACIO, Nicodemus
298	791	PANDY, Percival
299	200	PANTON, Robert Edward
300	1017	PANDY, Journett Herman
301	294	PARKS, Desmond Frederick
302	277	PARKS, James Nathaniel
303	1118	PASCASCTO, Coddrington Erold
304	1132	PERZOLD, Stanley Emanuel
305	2181	PEREZ, Gabriel
306	2127	POLLARD, Arthur
307	2275	PRINCE, Henry
308	2363	PETERS, James
309	2709	PETILLO, Dillon
310	1115	PILGRIM, Alonzo Percival
311	2171	POLLARD, Castro Calistro
312	2679	PENTILLO, Margarito
313	2692	PETILLO, Patrocino
314	2814	PANTING, John
315	1129	PITTS, Frederick Edward
316	1248	PYKE, Solomon
317	2762	REYES, Evarido
318	2306	RICHARD, William E.
319	1148	RAYMOND, James Nathaniel
320	823	RAFAEL, Cayatano
321	183	RAMOS, Fransisco
322	2807	REYNOLDS, Herbert
323	2310	RICHARDS, Pascual
324	1065	REYNOLDS, Donald K.
325	2559	REYNOLDS, Pamzey
326	2613	RIVERS, Adolphus
327	1100	RAYMOND, John
328	728	ROBINSON, James
329	2497	RICHARDSON, Ethelred
330	571	RIVERROLL, Apolonio
331	462	ROCHES, Jacob
332	480	ROSE, Robert Alexander
333	496	RODRIQUEZ, Paul
334	932	SABAL, John

335	2527	SALAZAR, Jacinto
336	566	SAMUELS, Sydney
337	415	SAMPSON, Daniel
338	2718	SALAM, Reinaldo
339	2390	SANCHEZ, Charles
340	2038	SHEPHERD, Thomas William
341	424	SHAW, Hubert Peter
342	2726	SELGADO, Nicomedes
343	2292	SIMPSON, Percival
344	552	SLUSHER, Clarence
345	304	SMITH, Nathaniel
346	2517	SMITH, Selvyn
247	2498	SMALL, Hugh Donald
348	578	SMITH, Thomas
349	2567	SOLIS, Herman
350	526	SOSA, Mateo
351	2263	SOSA, Valentin
352	2525	SPENCE, Rudolph
353	2299	STEVANS, Ivan Percival
354	38	STAINE, Joseph
355	459	SUAZO, Crispin
356	434	SWASEY, Cecil
357	2375	THOMPSON, Calbert
358	860	THURTON, Charles
359	1112	THURTON, Walrick
360	2304	TIABO, James
361	2565	THOMPSON, Crispin
362	2799	TORRES, Aureio
363	2400	TORRES, Christopher
364	2441	TUCKER, Henry
365	2440	TUCKER, Samuel
366	2458	UNDERWOOD, Berthan
367	334	UNDERWOOD, Laurence
368	2415	USHER, William
369	549	USHER, Cardinal
370	151	USHER, Cleophus
371	856	VALERIO, Aparicio
372	523	VERA, Adolfe
373	2763	VASQUEZ, Adolfo
374	2060	VERGO, Joseph A.
375	2309	VALENCIA, Suth
376	2058	VERNON, Ambrose, H.
377	2092	VERNON, Vincente
378	212	VERNON, Algernon Harrington
379	672	VICENTE, Marshall
380	376	VELASQUEZ, Patrucinio Alonzo
381	2288	VERNON, Edwin
382	2139	VILLANUEVA, Luciano
383	2196	WADE, Frederick

384	1236	WADE, John
385	124	WARREN, George Joseph
386	63	WEBSTER, Stephen Emanuel
387	645	WITTY, Epifanio
388	2011	WELCOME, Donald C.
389	2267	WONG, Manuel
390	2465	WHYTE, Frederick
391	2307	WADE, Hubert
392	2141	WADE, Henry
393	2052	WHITE, Winston
394	2555	WILLIAMS, Felix
395	302	WILLIS, Ralph
396	1227	WADE, Stephen
397	2632	WIGHT, Samuel Joseph
398	623	WALTER, Calbert
399	518	WHITE, Arthur
400	698	WILLIAMS, Maurice
401	624	WILLIAMS, Thomas
402	2653	WILLIAMS, Alfred
403	2337	WILLIAMS, Carl
404	2722	WOO S, Hayman
405	2813	YAMA, Dionicio A.
406	2646	YE, Pedro
407	2348	YOUNG, Egbert
408	2290	YOUNG, Peter
409	1221	YOUNG, Norman
410	2009	YSAGUIRRE, Louis
411	217	ZUNIGA, Ciracio
412	911	ZUNIGA, Cresencio
413	2795	ZUNIGA, Louis
414	457	ZUNIGA, Apolonio
415	543	ZELAYA, Francis Alexander